KINDLING WATCH-FIRES:

BEING A BRIEF SKETCH OF

THE LIFE OF

REV. VIVIAN A. DAKE

By

IDA DAKE PARSONS

First Fruits Press
Wilmore, Kentucky
c2016

Kindling watch-fires: being a brief sketch of the life of Rev. Vivian A. Dake,
By Ida Dake Parsons

First Fruits Press, ©2016

Previously published by the Free Methodist Publishing House, ©1915

ISBN: 9781621714866 (print) 9781621714873 (digital) 9781621714880 (kindle)

Digital version at http:http://place.asburyseminary.edu/freemethodistbooks/11/

For all other uses, contact:

First Fruits Press
B.L. Fisher Library
Asbury Theological Seminary
204 N. Lexington Ave.
Wilmore, KY 40390
http://place.asburyseminary.edu/firstfruits

Parsons, Ida Dake.
    Kindling watch-fires : being a brief sketch of the life of Rev. Vivian A.
    Dake, together with a compilation of selections from his writings, sermons,
    and poems, to which is appended a few of his best songs with the music /
    by Mrs. Ida Dake Parsons.
        209 [9] pages.: portraits; 21 cm.
    Wilmore, Kentucky : First Fruits Press, © 2016.
    Reprint. Previously published: Chicago: Free Methodist Publishing House,
    © 1915.
    ISBN: 9781621714866 (paperback)
    1. Dake, Vivian A. (Vivian Adelbert) 1854-1892. 2. Free Methodist Church
    of North America--Clergy--Biography. I. Title.

BX8419. D3 P3 2016   287.97

Cover design by Jonathan Ramsay

asburyseminary.edu
800.2ASBURY
204 North Lexington Avenue
Wilmore, Kentucky 40390

First Fruits
THE ACADEMIC OPEN PRESS OF ASBURY SEMINARY

First Fruits Press
The Academic Open Press of Asbury Theological Seminary
204 N. Lexington Ave., Wilmore, KY 40390
859-858-2236
first.fruits@asburyseminary.edu
asbury.to/firstfruits

KINDLING WATCH-FIRES

REV. VIVIAN A. DAKE

KINDLING WATCH-FIRES

Being a Brief Sketch of the
LIFE OF
REV. VIVIAN A. DAKE

Together with a Compilation of Selections from his
Writings, Sermons, and Poems, to which is
appended a few of his best Songs with
the Music

By
MRS. IDA DAKE PARSONS

PUBLISHED FOR THE AUTHOR

FREE METHODIST PUBLISHING HOUSE
CHICAGO, ILLINOIS
1915

DEDICATED

to our three daughters, Mary, Carrie, and Ruth, with the earnest prayer that they may be filled with that holy enthu-siasm and passion for souls which characterized their father.

INTRODUCTION

When I was asked by Mrs. Ida Dake Parsons if I thought a book containing the writings, sermons and poems of Rev. V. A. Dake would be a success, I did not regard the suggestion favorably. I feared that since one book giving an account of his life had been issued, another would not meet with sufficient success to warrant publication. But after reading the manuscript, and having received from it an inspiration to be a holier man, to be more earnest in preaching the gospel and in carrying forward the work of God, I felt that the world needed the book, and consented to assist the author in getting it out.

It was my privilege to be closely associated with Brother Dake for several years. He made my office in Chicago his headquarters. I learned that his private life was spotless. He was "an Israelite indeed in whom was no guile." He was a man of much prayer; he would allow nothing to deprive him of his secret, or rather private (for when the Lord blest him his shouts could be heard a long distance), devotions. His faith was of that stalwart sort that did not depend on circumstances or appearances.

On one occasion he came in from an absence of some time and opened and read his mail. He soon began to shout and praise the Lord. I asked him if his mail contained good news. He said, "No—quite to the contrary." Some of his workers had left the field and gone home. One had fallen into disgrace and had been discontinued, and some other discouraging things had happened which I do not remember. He said it was the worst situation he had encountered since his Band work had been started.

I asked, Why do you rejoice when things are going so discouragingly? "I rejoice," said he, "because Father's at the helm, and notwithstanding all these things the work will go on, and we shall have victory."

The new book will be a tonic to faith, an inspiration to prayer, and an encouragement to undertake large and difficult things for the kingdom of Christ.

T. B. ARNOLD.

CONTENTS

KINDLING WATCH-FIRES

CHAPTER I

BIOGRAPHICAL

If "to live in hearts we leave behind is not to die," then Vivian A. Dake still lives in the memory of thousands, "embalmed by love and garlanded with affection." Although almost a quarter of a century has passed since the mystic veil receded and his noble spirit went to be with God, yet his works still praise him, and his burning message, both in word and song, is richly owned and blessed of God in the salvation of souls and in the strengthening of believers.

No marble shaft has been erected to perpetuate his memory. He needs none. His name and his counsel are chiseled on the tablets of too many hearts to need the aid of bronze or marble to perpetuate them. And yet, just because he obtained such a good report, just because his commanding personality is woven into the web of our denominational traditions, just because the earth and the kingdom are the poorer for his going home, it is fitting that his teachings, both by precept and example, be preserved for future generations. "Weighed in the flawless balances of heaven, there are results and values here that dwarf all other accomplishment. And he whose recollection we treasure is to be classed among this elect company. His was one of those individualities which are exceptional in the Christian circle, because of peculiar vir-

tues and endowments. Men such as he cannot be mustered
into regiments; they are too few."

Of beautiful disposition, endowed with uncommon
capacities and clothed with humility, absolutely surrendered to the Lord's use, he became one of the most remarkable soul-winners and princely leaders the church
has known.

HOME LIFE AND EARLY CHILDHOOD

Vivian Adelbert Dake was the eldest of five children
born to the Rev. Jonathan Woodcock Dake and his excellent wife, Althelia Merrill Dake. He first saw the light of
day, February 9, 1854, in the little town of Oregon, Ogle
county, Illinois. He was fortunate in the influence of a home
which was truly a Bethel—a place where God delighted to
dwell, and he could say with Obadiah of old, "I, thy servant, fear the Lord from my youth up." He was truly a
child of the church. When the controversy in the Methodist
Episcopal church on the subject of holiness reached its
climax in 1859, among those who were compelled to leave
the church for conscience' sake was the Rev. J. W. Dake.
For a number of years he had been a preacher of righteousness, full of faith and of the Holy Ghost, whose labors God
was pleased to honor with success. He was in fullest
sympathy with the teachings of Dr. Redfield, which agreed
with those of the honored founder of Methodism, and in
1860, when it became necessary to organize another religious society, he and his wife were enrolled as charter
members of the Free Methodist church. Thus Vivian, who
was then but six years of age, grew up in the church, im-
bibed its principles, loved them, honored them, and fought
his last battle for holiness under its banner.

True to their vows of consecration, Mr. and Mrs. Dake
brought up their children in the nurture and admonition

of the Lord. These children, Vivian, Mary, Flora, Charles, and Gilbert, were early led in the paths of rectitude and, while yet at a tender age, they felt God's hand upon them and yielded to His call. From infancy they prayed at the family altar where the Shekinah dwelt continually. At the age of nine Vivian was clearly converted to God. But, amid the trials attendant upon childhood and the constant change of companions caused by the itinerant life of his parents, he did not keep his experience in grace. Though he never became hardened in sin, like so many American youths, yet there were times when his wild propensities were indulged. But when corrected, his heart would be touched; he would burst into tears, throw his arms about his parents' necks and beg forgiveness.

SCHOOL LIFE

Although Mr. and Mrs. Dake were solicitous concerning the needful preparation for Vivian's life-work, yet their circumstances were such as to make it utterly impossible for them to give him an education. But "God's merciful providence overruled this obstacle and opened a way which led to the needed fields of knowledge." At a camp-meeting held in Sheffield, Illinois, in August, 1867, an incident occurred, of which the late Bishop B. T. Roberts wrote, and which beautifully tells the story of God's overruling providence in matters concerning His children. It was while he was raising money to erect buildings for the seminary at North Chili, New York. "One of the first who gave," says Mr. Roberts, "was a bashful boy of about twelve or thirteen, who had outgrown his clothes. As, trembling, he placed a ten-cent piece in my hand, a thrill went over me like a gentle shock of electricity and a voice said, 'If the children take such an interest, the school will be a success.' In 1870, after the school was in successful operation, I mentioned this circumstance at a camp-meeting in New York. Mrs. Roberts said, 'This boy is the son of a Free Methodist preacher in poor circumstances, getting a scanty support. Will not some one here send him to school?' At the close of the meeting Mrs. Joseph Mackey, of New York, said, 'Send for him to go to school, and I will pay his bills.'

When the news reached him that he could get an education he was in the field hoeing corn. To express his joy, he turned a somersault and stood on his head. He came to our school at Chili, a bright, uncultivated, unconverted boy, thirsting for knowledge, ambitious to learn.

Soon after entering school on February 23, 1872, he was wonderfully reclaimed. In seeking for pardon, "the determination which was so prominent in the man was manifest in the boy,—as, after vainly seeking peace for some time, he made the expression while on his knees: 'I'll stay here till I bleach my bones, or find pardon.' This resolution made him desperate and enabled him to seize the prize. 'The Kingdom of heaven suffereth violence, and the violent take it by force.' His joy knew no bounds. He shouted and praised God with a loud voice, and even leaped for joy."

Of his Christian experience Brother Roberts bore the following testimony: "His religion was not of the quiet, unemphatic kind. The love of Christ was like fire shut up in his bones. With others he went from house to house wherever it was acceptable, prayed, exhorted, and endeavored to win souls to Christ and to help them on in the kingdom of grace. After graduating at Chili Seminary, he entered Rochester University. He maintained a creditable standing in his studies and not only kept his religious fervor, but his ardor for soul-saving became so intense that he could not stay and finish his collegiate course, so after completing three terms in the University,

he began his life-work as a minister of the gospel by helping his father in revival meetings. He preached his first
sermon, July 12, 1874, at Jefferson, Iowa. The Lord rewarded his labors by saving one sister and sanctifying
another. On August ninth he had the privilege of filling his father's appointments for the first time, and was
much helped of the Lord. He had a dread of formalism,
and he prayed most earnestly for the Lord to keep him all
aflame with the fire of the Holy Ghost. He maintained
that he would rather have the "gift of devil-dislodging
faith than all the learning that can be acquired in earth's
schools."

On September fifth he made the following entry in
his diary: "We had a blessed time in our Big Woods grove-
meeting to-day. I preached my first sermon in the woods
and felt the help of the Spirit. A lady from W. was
gloriously saved. Have been thinking of late that perhaps I made a mistake in leaving the University so soon,
and while talking with God about it one day I told Him
that if, on the next Monday, when I returned to Waterloo,
I should find some money in the office to help me, I would
take it as an indication of His will for me to return. On
arriving in town I went at once to the post-office. There
I found a letter containing a money order and a slip of
paper on which was written: 'This is to aid you to return
to College.' Surely the ways of the Lord are past finding
out. I also received a letter saying that Emory Coleman,
for whom I had been praying for a year, was converted.
Praise the Lord for this!"

In due time he returned to the University, and was soon
a vital part of the religious life at that place. He was also
interested in the Crusade movement that was sweeping the
country at that time, and was so deeply impressed with
the "mobbing of a temperance lecturer on the streets of
Rochester, New York, by a lot of infuriated liquor men,
whose actions indicated the awful power that rum holds

in our land," that he wrote: "God speed the cause of prohibition!"

Soon after this he had the privilege of visiting Chili Seminary, his "spiritual birth place, where old things passed away and all things became new." To him salvation seemed written wherever his eyes rested. The place and the people never seemed dearer to him than they did at that time. As he looked around the walls, "rendered sacred by many associations and recollections," this beautiful quotation rushed upon him with new force: "There is a spot to me more dear than native vale or mountain. 'Tis where I first my Savior found, where I was first forgiven."

A distinguishing trait that characterized Vivian Dake was true, moral courage. "Fearless and free, firm-rooted in his beliefs, he set his course by the polar star of duty, and held to that without swerving." Even while at the University there was no compromise with him. While a student there the boys of his society wished him to join them in getting up a supper. It was a trying time, but the Lord helped him to stand by his principles, "and in spite of importunity, scolding and ridicule," he quietly said, "No. I'll not tone down for any one, but I'll shout on as I began."

He assisted in a tent meeting at Churchville, New York, which proved to be his first battle-ground. "Brother Roberts opened the tent meeting, with Brothers Dake, Mark Harrison, and Philip Hanna assisting. At this meeting a man came rushing to the altar where his wife was groaning and pleading for mercy, and dragged her away. A week later she had the privilege of leading him to the same altar, where he found glorious deliverance from his sins."

Their next meeting was in the tent at Brockport, where a number were saved. One of the converts was a young Catholic lady. Speaking of her conversion, he says, under date of September first: "It made her mother threaten to kill her. In the afternoon her mother met me, and such a storm of abuse it was never my lot to receive before.

"Rumors kept coming in that the Catholics were going to tear the tent down, but at the Democratic ratification meeting only two salutes were fired, when an explosion took place and two Catholics were dangerously injured. One had his arm torn off and was badly burned; the other had his eyes blown out, his skull fractured, his hand torn off and his face and body badly burned. These two young men were the ring leaders of the mob who proposed to tear down the tent. The people here regard the accident as a direct visitation from God. The tent was unmolested. The meeting soon closed, much good having been done."

At the close of this meeting he returned to the College at Rochester where he stayed but two weeks. Then, as Brother Roberts says: "His love for souls was so predominant that he could not be persuaded to remain longer in College, but started for Iowa where he intended to enter the ministry." He stopped a week at Spring Arbor, Michigan, where he visited Lenna Bailey, daughter of a former Editor of the *Free Methodist,* to whom he had been engaged. In company with her and her mother he started for his home, where they were to be married, stopping at the Illinois conference which was then in session at Aurora, Illinois. Here he was appointed to the St. Charles circuit, but went on to his parents' home in Birmingham, Iowa, where in a few days he was married by his father to Miss Bailey. She was very frail, having lung trouble, and was kept from the grave only by the special interposition of Providence.

EARLY MINISTRY

On account of his wife's ill health, he was unable to take his appointment at St. Charles circuit, but instead took work in Iowa on the Birmingham and Fairfield circuit, as junior preacher with the Rev. R. S. Ellis. In November he began to assist Brother Ellis in a revival at Union, Iowa, in which eighteen souls were saved in two weeks, some of whom were the clearest conversions he ever saw. From his diary we quote: "I love the work of the Lord. I am dying to things of time and sense. Oh, I would rather die than exalt myself. I will live humble. I long for more of the life of Jesus. I am determined to obey God at any cost."

So greatly did God bless him in walking humbly before him, that when his precious wife slipped away from him and a host of loved ones, to be with Jesus, on the morning of December 20, 1876, he found through all this that his "bleeding heart was strengthened by the grace and power of God," and heavy though the stroke seemed, he could say that there was not a murmur in his heart. Through all this his love for souls never wavered, and as soon as it was possible he returned to Fairfield, where God immediately began to bless and reward his labors with precious souls. On January 4, 1877, he wrote in his journal: "After coming back from the funeral of my precious Lenna, I got a new hold of God for the work. God greatly helped me in preaching. I never felt more of His power than this evening. Five were seeking, two of whom were clearly saved. While preaching I felt like leaving the stand and going down the aisle. I felt much of the presence of God while doing so." Were we to continue to quote from his journal we would find his labors bearing rich fruitage for the Lord of the harvest. It was ever so, and what seems so precious is that a thorough work was accomplished through the blessed Holy Spirit that has stood the test of time, and we are assured will also stand the test of eternity.

At the Blakesbury camp-meeting, held in the following July, God came in great power during a sermon on holiness, after which Mr. Dake exhorted and invited seekers to the altar. In a moment the altar was crowded and soon all but one were saved. Again, others came and they were saved; still others came, and this time the altar was swept clean, all having been saved or sanctified.

The conference of 1877 appointed him to the Walker circuit. On January 30, 1878, he was united in marriage to Miss Ida May Campbell (the writer of this sketch), of Fairfield, Iowa, by the Rev. R. Gilbert. He remained on this circuit two years, where his labors were abundant and a large ingathering of souls was accomplished. While still there, on February 8, 1879, he wrote: "To-morrow I will be twenty-five years old; a quarter of a century. God only knows whether or not it shall be doubled. Should it be, I pledge myself to spend it in blowing the gospel trumpet with no uncertain sound." He held a short meeting at B. on this work, at which thirty were saved and twenty-eight sanctified, with much conviction through the country and prejudice cleared away. It will take eternity to tell the good done through the seed sown on his circuits, which were always doubled in size before the year was out. God was fitting him up for broader fields, into which He would soon lead him, where his wonderful powers could be fully exercised.

LABORS ON WATERLOO AND CEDAR FALLS CIRCUITS

The conference of 1879 sent him to Waterloo circuit. Here he remained two years. The second year Rev. J. M. Reilly was sent to help him as junior preacher. The latter is our authority for the statement that about one hun-

dred souls were saved this second year, and the work so
extended that it was necessary for the conference of 1881
to make a division, Brother Dake being sent to Cedar
Falls. Brother Reilly speaks of him in this early stage of
his ministry thus: "As a pastor, he was thorough, and
dealt faithfully with his people. He made himself at
home among them, whether at their houses, or in their
fields, or wherever they were. I have known him a number of times to take off his coat and help in the harvest or
hay field, while he talked with the men about their souls,
and before leaving he would kneel with them in the field,
and get blest with them in prayer."

He seems from the very first to have taken a stand with
the primitive church fathers in getting everybody at work
and thus multiplying their talents and usefulness. One of
his letters to the *Free Methodist* at this time closes with
these words: "I saw some appeals in the paper to this
effect: 'PREACHERS! We want PREACHERS!' I
thought while reading it, What is that man doing? There
are preachers buried in the graves of sin everywhere. If
we want preachers we must dig them out. I believe if
some of our conferences that are appealing so loudly for
help to the outside world would set small and great to
work within their bounds they would soon be sending
laborers into the great outside harvest field. The fisher-
men, shepherds and publicans, they seem afraid to send
out.

"We need some fathers in Israel, like Paul, Wesley, and
Asbury, superintendents or chairmen, to direct on the
field of battle, but not to do all the work. Don't be afraid
of the boys and girls; send them out; give them your help
and blessing, and their freshness, strength and zeal, united
with your experience and wisdom, will gain the battle.
I am young in experience, but I find those everywhere who
want to work, and only need encouragement to become
efficient. If we go to work ourselves and give others a

chance the chariot will roll on. 'Say not ye, There are yet four months, and then cometh harvest? Lift up your eyes, and look on the fields; for they are white already to harvest.' "

On August 11, 1881, we were caused to pass through a severe bereavement in the death of our only child, a dear baby boy, twenty-two months old. Mr. Dake records it thus: "My little darling Bertie is no more. He passed away easily. Another strand joined to the cable that pulls me heavenward; yet, by God's grace, wife and I are enabled to say, 'The will of the Lord be done.' Amid the blinding tears, a vision of a cherub singing redemption's song, cheers our hearts. Oh, glory to God! My heart bleeds and yet triumphs. As we came back from the funeral, how lonely the home appeared. It seemed almost that I could see Bertie's bright eyes peering through the lattice work of the porch, or hear the patter of his feet, or the sweet music of his voice, saying, 'Papa! Papa!' Hushed forever on earth, but in heaven—oh, yes, we shall see him again." Our home, so clouded by this stroke, was brightened by the advent, on December fifteenth, of a daughter whom we called Mary.

REMARKABLE CAMP-MEETING AT HEBRON, MINNESOTA

In the fall of 1881, Mr. Dake was again sent to Cedar Falls and Waterloo, where he "kept revival fires burning all around him." The summer following he was invited to assist in a camp-meeting at Hebron, Minnesota. Concerning this meeting we quote from his journal:

"June 7th. I started for Hebron, Minnesota, this forenoon. I found William R. Cusick on the train and we proceeded together toward Mankato. First our way was over broad, level prairies, then we struck the Minnesota River, and winding around hills, crossing rivers, or leaping between overhanging bluffs lined with forest trees, we finally reached Mankato. It is a quiet city, scattered widely over the bluffs, which are numerous along the river. Here is where twenty-seven Indians, convicted of murder in the Sioux massacre of 1862, were all hanged at one drop of the trap. From Mankato, we drove ten miles over the roughest of roads to Hebron."

"June 8th. Well, here I am in this historic country. Through this very forest roamed the wild Sioux Indian. The surges of the terrible massacre rolled within a few miles of this place. New Ulm, eighteen miles northwest, was half destroyed by the Indians. The same summer, and preceding the massacre, the inhabitants of New Ulm dragged an effigy of the Savior through the streets and burned it. Then came the scourge of God—the Indians. Last summer the same town was literally torn to pieces by a cyclone, thirty or more people were killed and about two hundred houses destroyed. Within a mile or two of this camp ground went the James brothers after their disastrous raid on Northfield. They stopped in various houses in this valley."

"Sabbath, June 11th. This has been one of the highest days I ever saw. I preached this morning. It was a time of solemn interest.

"Brother Ellis preached in the afternoon. Twenty-two crowded to the altar. Oh, it was wonderful! Many were saved. The exact number I do not know. All classes were crying for mercy. In the evening Brother Cusick preached a powerful sermon; twenty-four came forward and again God's awful power shook Israel's camp."

He modestly omits in his record of this day what is stated by our informant, that he exhorted with much help after Brother C's evening sermon. In the course of his

exhortation he quoted with great feeling and accuracy the
following words from Pollok's "Course of Time":

> "Eternal Justice! sons
> Of God! tell me, if ye can tell, what then
> I saw, what then I heard? Wide was the place,
> And deep as wide, and ruinous as deep.
> Beneath, I saw a lake of burning fire,
> With tempest tossed perpetually, and still
> The waves of fiery darkness 'gainst the rocks
> Of dark damnation broke, and music made
> Of melancholy sort; and overhead,
> And all around, wind warred with wind, storm howled
> To storm, and lightning, forked lightning crossed,
> And thunder answered thunder, muttering sounds
> Of sullen wrath; and far as sight could pierce,
> Or down descend in caves of hopeless depth,
> Through all that dungeon of unfading fire,
> I saw most miserable beings walk,
> Burning continually, yet unconsumed;
> Forever wasting, yet enduring still;
> Dying perpetually, yet never dead.
> Some wandered lonely in the desert flames,
> And some in fell encounter fiercely met,
> With curses loud, and blasphemies, that made
> The cheek of darkness pale; and as they fought,
> And cursed, and gnashed their teeth, and wished to die,
> Their hollow eyes did utter streams of woe.
> And there were groans that ended not, and sighs
> That always sighed, and tears that ever wept,
> And ever fell, but not in Mercy's sight.
> And Sorrow, and Repentance, and Despair,
> Among them walked, and to their thirsty lips
> Presented frequent cups of burning gall.
> And as I listened, I heard these beings curse
> Almighty God, and curse the Lamb, and curse
> The earth, the resurrection morn, and seek,
> And ever vainly seek, for utter death;
> And to their everlasting anguish still,
> The thunders from above responding spoke
> These words, which, through the caverns of perdition
> Forlornly echoing, fell on every ear:
> 'Ye knew your duty, but ye did it not.' "

The effect was awful as these last words were slowly repeated. The speaker is described as presenting a most striking appearance during this exhortation, forgetful of all else but the awful subject in hand and the concourse of eternity-bound mortals before him. He paced back and forth on the platform, occasionally brushing back his hair with a gesture peculiar to himself, while his words poured forth like a burning torrent. Many trembled while conviction took hold of them.

From his journal of June twelfth, we quote: "The love-feast ran till noon to-day. It was a time of blessing. Nineteen were forward this afternoon and many to-night."

"June 13th. The scenes of yesterday were repeated to-day with increased power. Love-feast again ran till nearly noon. In the altar service which followed many sought and found the Lord. A noble looking young man, who is the ringleader of the young men in these parts, was converted and leaped for joy. Brother Cusick preached one of his characteristic sermons in the afternoon. In the evening Brother Ellis was helped in preaching. The altar was again crowded, there being two rows of seekers. Young ladies were seeking for brothers in the large and heart-stricken congregation. They threw themselves into each others arms and sobbed and groaned and prayed until mercy came.

"Three men and their wives, the young men's father and mother and the father of one of the wives, were all at the altar at once. Oh, it was grand! How the cause of God triumphed. I found no one who spoke against the meeting. All seemed alike struck by the awful power of our great God. It began to storm while opening the doors of the church this evening. Seventeen joined, besides Henrietta Muzzy, who had been the only Free Methodist in the country, and who was the means under God of having the camp-meeting here. After this the young man, formerly the ringleader in the devil's ranks, who was saved in the morning, began to call on the young men to come to Jesus. After a while ten or fifteen were at the altar, many of whom were grandly saved.

"It surpasses words to tell of the scenes of these hours. Angels and saints united in rejoicing over these new-born souls. Sinners trembled and hell shook. Oh, bless my God forever! At two-thirty in the morning I took seven more into the church, all young people, most of whom had been saved since the doors were opened in the evening. Oh, this clean work of salvation! I will preach and exemplify it while I live."

In his journal, July fourth, we read: "Never in my life was I so helped of God in preaching. Took eighteen into the church this morning, making a total of fifty-four. A good meeting in the afternoon; about forty seeking the Lord. In the evening, over fifty crowded to the altar, many of whom were clearly saved or sanctified. Oh, the wondrous display of God's power!"

That was the last day of the camp-meeting, and words are too weak to describe the scenes of power and glory witnessed that day and night. This meeting was a small one, a small one as regards numbers, there being less than a dozen tents up and only about seven preachers, and they mostly boys, but it was mighty in its results.

"July 9th. Here I am on my own circuit again. A Sabbath of salvation. In the evening at the Falls there were nine or ten forward and five saved; five joined the class on probation. 'Oh, praise the Lord, for He is good!' "

"July 12th. Spent the day mostly visiting, praying, and settling up my affairs. I go to Minnesota to-morrow. My official board has agreed to let me go out in several meetings until conference."

"July 14th. Wife and I came on to Mankato to-day.

Found Brother H. waiting to carry us to Hebron. In due time we reached the church. Had a salvation time. A good many forward."

"July 16th. This was one of the days of the Son of Man.' I baptized a good many this afternoon and took eight more into the church this evening. The meeting tonight ran until 1:30. The conflicts, fears, and doubts are all past and the young converts are all encouraged and victorious. As the meeting had continued in the Spirit from the first, strong opposition began to spring up. There had been a clean sweep of the tobacco, fashion and secrecy idols."

Some who had left all to follow Jesus and engage in the work for souls were strongly opposed by friends, and much effort was made to turn them from their course, but all to no avail. They pursued their way with joy, and now after ten years have elapsed, we find some of them true to their calling and laboring faithfully in the Lord's harvest. The meeting closed about the first of August, after having swept on with little abatement for nearly three months. It was during this meeting that he wrote the first of his songs.

We give it in this connection:

MY CROSS

O my cross! my dreaded cross,
    On which I die to live!
I take my cross, count all things loss,
    And life divine receive.

O my cross! my sev'ring cross,
    That me from all divides!
While heart-strings break for my Lord's sake,
    I, too, am crucified.

O my cross! my helpful cross!
   I gladly bear, and lo,
With wings I rise up to the skies!
   My cross, it lifts me so.

O my cross! my conqu'ring cross!
   By thee I overcome;
With victor's shout, the earth about,
   I fly till work is done.

O my cross! my heavenly cross!
   That fairer land I see
By faith's clear eye from Pisgah high,
   I pant at Home to be.

O my cross! not thine but mine;
   I clasp thee to my breast;
And nought shall part thee from my heart,
   Till I with Thee shall rest.

O my cross! our toils soon o'er
   Shall never be forgot;
By thee through pain rich joys I gain,
   A crown shall be my lot.

O my crown! O bliss complete!
   No conqueror's brow shall wear
A crown so bright, outshining light,
   As by the cross I'll bear.

MR. DAKE REMOVES TO MINNESOTA

We left Mankato September first, to attend the Iowa conference, which convened at Cedar Falls, September sixth. We are indebted to Brother Reilly for the following: "In the fall of 1882, Brother Dake, with a good deal of emotion, expressed his convictions to take a transfer to the Minnesota and Northern Iowa conference. He was granted the privilege of following his convictions in the matter, and was appointed by that conference as evangelist, to work which had formerly occupied two men, holding twenty-two meetings each quarter.

During the year a vacancy in the office of chairman occurred and Mr. Dake was chosen to fill the vacancy. The next year he was elected chairman of the three districts of which the conference was composed.

At this time Mr. Dake says: "Oh, what openings all through the northwest; beautiful towns springing up all around. Who will enter them? This district is thoroughly awakened. The preachers are as teachable as children. All through our conference they bear with my infirmities, give me encouraging words and send me on my way rejoicing. We are united. I know not of a bar or schism, and so unitedly we propose to take this land for God. This is the year of victory. We have slept in ease as long as we will. And the preachers of this conference are terribly in earnest to see men saved. Hell shall give way."

But the work of this year was too much for him and his body began to break down under it. Under his incessant labors his throat and lungs began to fail, so that when conference came in the fall of 1884, there was a fear that his earthly career would soon be ended, Nevertheless, the brethren again elected him as chairman of the three districts. Rev. T. B. Arnold, being present and seeing his worn-out condition, proposed for him a vacation. He next made a strong appeal to the people for a contribution to help send him away for a short season that he might rest and gain strength for future labors. They responded generously, and at the close of the conference, after having resigned his chairmanship, we accompanied Brother Arnold to Chicago. From thence we went on to the Michigan conference, where he was persuaded to take the Spring Arbor charge, preaching what he could on Sabbaths, but was to hold no revivals before winter or until he was able. As soon as he could he went down to Jackson to help Sister W. in a meeting. He says: "While there in Brother Bradfield's house, I asked Brother Stilwell to pray for my body. He did so, and the power of God struck me and went through my body from my head to my feet, and I was healed. Hallelujah, it was glorious! I began immediately to be more active."

CHAPTER II

THE PENTECOSTAL BAND WORK

At this time God began to lay the Pentecost Band work on him. He saw many of our young people, some of whom possessed great natural talents, sitting idly by, doing nothing for the Master, while the circuit preacher was left to do all that was to be done. He was grieved to see many of these young people either leave the church to labor in the Salvation Army (a work which he did not consider sufficiently deep and thorough, though possessing many admirable traits), or live much of the time void of a clear experience, or become entirely backslidden. The name was suggested to him because it appeared to be a return to primitive Pentecost methods, for in the revival at Pentecost converts as well as preachers engaged in spreading the gospel. This is why he was so loath to give up the name of "Pentecost Band" when requested to do so by some. "For," said he, "I feel our name was God-given. I saw," he writes, "the honors of the church. I was wanted in three different conferences to take the chairmanship. I was also wanted as editor of the *Free Methodist* and to take charge of either of two of the seminaries. To go into Band work I saw was the way of the cross, the way of reproach and shame. I knew many of my friends would turn from me, yet God seemed holding me to it." About this time he received the following letter from Superintendent B. T. Roberts:

North Chili, Monroe Co., N. Y., July 31, 1885.
My Dear Son in the Gospel:
Organize your Bands. Push out. Be as aggressive as the

Salvation Army, but more holy, more serious and have no nonsense about it. Let the Holy Spirit take the place of tambourines to draw the people. * * * We must not let the Free Methodist church become a feeble imitation of the M. E. church.

Yours affectionately,

B. T. ROBERTS.

From the beginning, the divine seal was on the movement. The first meetings broke out in power, and multitudes "which sat in darkness" and in the shadow of death "saw great light." Young people of both sexes from their farms, shops, schoolrooms, etc., applied for places in the work. Other meetings were soon commenced, and thus the work expanded.

Mr. Dake did not deem it necessary for these workers to be educated in science, literature, or even theology, before entering the Lord's harvest field. Being a scholar himself and seeing the value of education, he did not under-value these acquirements, but endeavored to inculcate a relish for study in these young people. But a polished education in a minister he did not consider essential to success in soul-saving. In this respect his work was appropriately named "Pentecost Band," as Christ, in choosing His disciples, and the apostolic church in the choice of its deacons, both seemed to lose sight of educational endowments, and sought for the fulness of faith and the Holy Ghost.

Thus he saw Zion's borders extended by utilizing the latent, though mighty, powers of these young people. Although under the ban of many who should have encouraged it, the work steadily increased until at his death nearly one hundred workers were in the field, laboring successfully for the lost; and we have no reason to believe that many of these workers would ever have done "the work of an evangelist" had not this movement been started.

Referring to the tests through which he was called to pass, on taking up Band work, he said in effect: "While in this strait, with self leaning to church aggrandizement and the Spirit drawing toward the cross, I saw there was love of position in my heart, and while holding myself open to the light of God I was more and more convinced that I did not enjoy the experience of holiness, and floods of astonishing light began to shine on me, in which, while reviewing my past experience, God showed me plainly I had never been dead indeed to self. I saw I had been much helped while keeping a blessed, clear experience in justification, but was mistaken in my experience in holiness. What I now saw to be the 'carnal mind' I had been calling temptation, humanity, etc. I had many struggles with these things and had often attained glorious victories, as I thought, over the temptation, and had gone on my way rejoicing. Now I saw, in light that was unmistakably from God, the depth of depravity in my heart. In my distress I went to God for deliverance from self. I confessed and deplored my carnal condition. Oh! what anguish of heart was mine, as I poured out my soul in pleading before God. A sense of self-abhorrence had taken possession of me. I would rather die than live in this condition. Oh! such pangs as I then felt, while crying out against 'the man of sin.' "

"Auntie Coon's faithful prayers and dealings were of great help to me in this critical hour. While honestly confessing, as Adam Clarke says, the 'sore of my soul' and heartily turning against the self nature within me, faith began to spring up, and a blessed sense of cleanness was mine without any special baptism. For two or three days longer I hung in the balance, hardly daring to claim that the cleansing blood had done the work, knowing how long I had been deceived, but glory to my King! as I looked up in faith and walked in humility, a baptism of fire, power, and glory soon fell on my soul that made me feel unearthly. An intense longing after souls, and an indescribable yearning for the lost, such as I had never before felt, now took possession of me and I began my life-work."

When, after much anxiety and great "searchings of heart," he saw his lack, he shrank not from an acknowledgment of the truth, even though he knew to what reproach and ridicule such an acknowledgment would expose him. It also manifested the candor and honesty of a magnanimous mind. Had many of his opposers done likewise, what untold blessings would have been conveyed to the church of Christ. Had his hearers done so generally, what a "cloud of witnesses" would have been added to her number.

This wonderful experience marked a new epoch in his life. We here give his own description of his dying to self, and receiving the fulness, as he expressed it, five years afterward in verse form, for the benefit of those who might be in like experience.

> I am coming to Mount Calvary,
> Where the Savior died for me,
> Stricken, burdened, I am coming;
> Crucify me, Lord, with Thee.
>
> CHORUS
> I am thirsting, I am dying,
> As I to Mount Calvary go;
> For the fulness I am crying,
> Wash me whiter than the snow.
>
> I have left the world behind me,
> Counting all its gain but dross;
> And myself I now am bringing
> To the altar of Thy cross.
>
> Oh! the blackness and the darkness
> In this sinful heart of mine;
> With the light upon me shining,
> Make, oh, make my heart like Thine.

Oh! the pangs of hell within me,
Oh! the striving to be free;
But the strong man, stronger dying,
Rends my heart, opposing Thee.

Let me die, O Cross of Calvary,
Nails and spear are welcome now;
And with agony unspoken,
To Thy death I gladly bow.

Hallelujah! it is finished,
Crucified with Christ I am,
And I'm cleansed from all defilement,
Through the all-atoning Lamb.

SECOND CHORUS
I am filled, oh, hallelujah!
As I from Mount Calvary go;
And my heart the blood now cleanses,
Whiter than the driven snow.

Pentecost with all its glory,
Power divine upon my soul;
On to victory, full of praises,
While eternal ages roll.

The Pentecostal Bands were now fairly started and doing good work in the field, to which he gave himself through them, without grudging, without stint, to the work of Christ. He had a Pauline conception of a soul-winner, and labored with a zeal that was like consuming fire. As the work done by the Bands has been fully described in "Life and Labors of Vivian A. Dake," by Thomas H. Nelson, from which we have taken many of our quotations, we will attempt no eulogy on them. The few articles here inserted will give the reader who does not know of the Band work some idea concerning it.

PENTECOSTAL BAND ANNUAL HARVEST HOME

This meeting began with an annual praise meeting on the evening of Friday, July 25. On that evening we had been five years in the Band work. It was a joyous time. The workers were there after a year's separation, and all were blessed and fired with the privilege of fellowship and the baptism of power. The following days until the thirtieth were spent in our annual workers' meeting and holding evening services. Many attended these services. The camp-meeting commenced July 30, and the saints came from a number of states around. We are made glad to meet Brother Warren Hames, of West Webster, N. Y.; Brother George Willard, from the Burg, and Brother A. C. Goodenough, from Rochester, N. Y. Brothers Hawkins and Showers, from the Pittsburgh conference, were present and were helped of the Spirit, and were very helpful to the workers. We asked them to come again. Brothers Flower and Davis, and Brother Whitcomb, pastor of the Second Methodist Episcopal church, Oshkosh, Wisconsin, were present, also Brothers Brooke, Christie, Ketels and W. M. Kelsey, of the Illinois conference; Brothers Colt, Sherman, Huston, Fleming, Bone, Bonham, Graham and Bruce, of the Central Illinois conference; Brothers Morrow and Ferguson, of the Wabash conference, and Brothers Easton, Brown, and Murphee, four young men traveling the new circuits raised up by the Bands; nearly all the Band workers, and Sisters Coon, Sutcliffe and Gates of the Rams Horn Band.

God was present. The ground was swept by the power of God. Very few left without cleansing. The groans of the dying commingled with the shouts of victory. Preachers and laymen were delivered from the carnal mind. Thorough work was done. Praise the Lord! About twenty were baptized and a number joined the Free Methodist church.

The missionary meetings were times of blessing. At the African missionary meeting $215.50 was paid and subscribed. Waves of glory came. Sisters Mattie E. North and Jennie Torrence, leaders of Band Number Nine, gave their experiences and announced themselves as ready for Africa. So mightily was the Spirit in the meeting that after the money had been raised the altar filled up with seekers and a number were converted.

There was $150 raised for the missions in Norway and Sweden. Brother and Sister Ulness and Hans Foss testified that they were called to this work. God was present and the Holy Ghost came. Fifty-five dollars was also raised for the Germany mission. All the expenses of the meeting were easily met. Fifty dollars was given on the tabernacle fund and thirty-five dollars toward plastering Morgan Street church.

The workers started out clean, almost to the last one. Glory to God! Oh, how our souls burn for the lost in every field! Brother Roberts wrote me some time since, asking if we could not send a Band to France. A brother writes for a Pentecost worker in England. The world stretches out its hands. "Where are the reapers?" As fast as they come and submit to hardships and tests on their obedience in the home field, we will help them to take their God-appointed posts in any land. Hallelujah!

PENTECOST BAND WORK

The work moves on gloriously. Pentecost Band Number Two has closed at Hanover with twenty-five clear conversions. A number joined the Free Methodist church. Number Three still sees souls saved in the tent. Glory! Hallelujah! If our good editor was out on the field of battle where some of us are, he would blow a blast that would make the dry bones rattle. Awake! Souls are perishing.

Where is the early Methodist pioneer spirit? Who lives out the spirit of the following lines?

"The love of Christ doth me constrain,
To seek the wandering souls of men;

With cries, entreaties, tears to save,
To snatch them from the gaping grave."

See the tide of popularity coming in on us. Rich **Free** Methodists are holding on to their thousands and the work of God is suffering. Judgment thunders will soon arouse us from our stupor. Judgment fires will consume our hoarded wealth and we will leave our thousands in time and, if we are not careful, we shall be beggars in eternity.

We need an advance all along the line. Superintendents, editors, chairmen, sound the alarm. Set the example. At what an infantile pace we are creeping along. Some conferences are losing ground, some are barely holding their own, while a few are gaining quite moderately. Years are rolling by like a forest before a cyclone. Men are going into eternity. The judgment is at hand. Oh, shall we not sing from the gulf to the lakes, from ocean to ocean,

"Only for souls, while the tear drops start;
Only for souls, though with aching heart.
Go friendships and pleasures; your death-knell tolls.
Only for souls, only for souls."

And the Pentecost Band will sing with all their strength in return,

"Only for souls, sing the Pentecost Band,
Only for souls, shout the victory grand.
The tidal wave's coming; triumphant it rolls.
Only for souls, only for souls."

Hallelujah! Glory!

ARRESTED

What for? For obeying the Savior's command, "Go out into the highways and hedges, and compel them to come in, that my house may be filled." When? In the nineteenth century, in the accumulated and focused light of this favored day of grace. Where? In this boasted land of liberty, under the shadow of churches and free schools, Christian ladies are hurried away to jail. In Braceville, Morris, Streator, and Ottawa, Illinois, has this happened.

But some say, "Why do you resist the powers that be?" For the same reason that Peter and John did, when they were straitly threatened and arrested while holding street meetings. (See Acts 3: 13-21 and 5: 15, 16.) We would not resist a just law. Where there is a law forbidding all gatherings on the streets, we respect the ordinance. But where they have none, and all the devil's side-shows are free to attract men hellward, we hold on our way even to prison and to death. "In the last days perilous times shall come." I find them in these days. But our God delivereth and rescueth. Some have wished us to sue the cities for false imprisonment; but we have not, so far, felt thus led. If God raises up defenders, we gladly accept of them; and if not, just as gladly suffer with our Jesus, who might have escaped His cup and baptism by yielding. We do not feel stubborn nor wilful, and when we hear there is trouble we always go to the mayor and request a corner; but if he refuses, we obey God and take the results. Brethren, pray for us.

ESTIMATES OF THE BAND WORK

Perhaps in no place up to that time had the opposition taken the form of false accusations and scandalous stories, as in Tuscola, Illinois. It was commenced by relatives of some of the converts from Camargo, six miles distant, who were violent in their opposition, and tireless in circulating slanderous reports of the work and workers. The junior Editor of a Tuscola paper, *The Review,* made himself a champion of these parties and began at once to publish a series of reports which perhaps were never equaled for falsehood, foulness, and calumny.

We would insert some of these articles, copies of which we have at hand, but we consider them unfit for publication. One extremely false and slanderous article of this kind, apparently from the pen of this Editor, appeared in the *St. Louis Republic*. We here give Superintendent B. T. Roberts' reply to the same:

A STRANGE SECT

In reading the article in the *St. Louis Republic* for December 24th, under the above heading, we were in doubt as to whether it was intended to be a statement of fact, or whether some aspiring youth was trying his 'prentice hand at wit and humor. But as it will doubtless be taken as true, we deem it proper to make a brief reply.

In general terms we say that the article in question is not only an exaggeration, a gross caricature, but for the most part it has not even the semblance of truth. The "Pentecost Band" is not a sect. It is not an "offshoot of the Mormon church." In short, every statement affecting the moral character or the religious standing of the Pentecost Bands, in the above article, is downright, unmitigated falsehood. The Pentecost Bands are Christian workers, moral, pious, godly, self-denying. They belong to the Free Methodist church. Each Band is composed of about four, either all young men, or all young women. They devote all their time and all their energy to getting sinners converted to God. Any one who will send thirty-five cents to the Free Methodist publishing house at Chicago, can obtain a Discipline and find out their doctrines. Their great offense is threefold.

First. They get men converted from beer and tobacco, as well as from other sins, and this makes saloonists mad.

Second. They get women converted from love of jewelry and fine dress.

Third. But worst of all, they get poor drunken, deluded Roman Catholics converted, and this stirs up the fiercest opposition against them. This is the sum of their offending.

B. T. ROBERTS,
Senior Superintendent (or Bishop) of the Free Methodist church,
104 Franklin street, Chicago, Illinois

But they were not without a host of friends and those who encouraged them in the work. We give one instance.

The following quotation from a published letter by Chairman T. J. Noland voices the mind of many with reference to Mr. Dake's work in connection with his Bands:

"May 15, 1890.

"I will just say here that I am a Free Methodist and would not encourage disloyalty in any one, nor in any sect or faction in the church. I do not believe there is a Free Methodist in the connection who knows me that would suspect me of such a thing. I have spent nine weeks altogether in connection with the Pentecost work, and in laboring with the workers, and I pronounce them, in the strictest sense of the term, Free Methodists. They are plain in apparel, more so than the generality of Free Methodists. They are strongly in favor of enforcing Discipline. They believe in conversion, also in entire sanctification, and enjoy these experiences. While they believe in salvation by faith, they do not believe in believing you have got it in order to get it.

"I would advise those who are afraid of their work, especially those tinctured with this 'naked faith' idea, to get one of these Bands to come on their work. It would pay you well to support a Band for six months, just to get straight on this idea. They are a blest people and believe in getting others blest. They use self-denial, in fasting often, and frequently in opening work they sleep in halls on naked boards, and live for days on small rations, sometimes nothing at all. Instead of trying to get people to believe they are Christians in order to become such, I have seen them question the conversion of those who professed to be converted among themselves, telling them to continue to seek until they knew they were converted.

"Now I have known among Free Methodists those who urge seekers to profession on the ground that if they had confessed their sins they were converted, forgiven, and had a right to testify to justification, witness or no witness. It does not seem strange to me that such persons should oppose these consecrated, self-denying saints who teach that when a soul is converted something takes place; that

" 'Heaven comes down our souls to greet,
And glory crowns the mercy-seat.'

"It does seem strange that some I have known in other years who taught this same theory are now the strongest friends to these Pentecost workers. Anyhow, if it is real it shows the power of truth over error. I question whether there is a conference in the Free Methodist church that has four or five preachers who would go into a place like Tuscola, Illinois, and hold meetings every night from eight to ten months, and rent a hall at eight dollars per month, and a house at six, and raise the money from their congregation to pay the rent, and also for their living. I think they would feel the need of more faith than they had when on their circuits, and but few there are who would try it at all.

"Another mark they have that shows to whom they belong and for whom they work. They are persecuted more than the common run of Free Methodists; the devil howls wherever they go. Now if there are any Free Methodists who are not persecuted, it is because they are not giving the kingdom of Satan much trouble. The Band at Tuscola was twice imprisoned, not for holding meetings on the streets, but for worshiping God aloud in their own hired hall.

*   *   *   *   *   *   *

"God forbid that I should ever oppose such self-sacrificing saints as I have found in these Pentecost workers. I have more than ten thousand square miles of territory in the northern end of the Wabash conference, and they are welcome to occupy every unoccupied mile of it."

The following excellent description of the last Harvest Home camp-meeting, which was written by a friendly Editor and published in his paper, will give our readers a good understanding of these Harvest Home meetings.

"The arrangement for public services was on the largest and most practical scale we ever saw. Three large tabernacles were placed together, making a space about one hundred feet wide, and fifty feet deep. This was seated inside and out, so as to accommodate two thousand people. The platform was seated to accommodate the preachers and workers—a hundred or more, as might be necessary.

"Besides the large tabernacle, two other large tents were pitched, one for the young ladies of the work, the other for the men. Several family tents were full, and with a number of small tents all made an easy equivalent to one hundred common tents on the ground. One of the buildings on the grounds was brought into use for a dining hall and managed by a delegation of boys and girls who took their turn about in washing dishes, cooking, waiting on the table, etc., so that there would not be any partiality shown and all might have a fair chance to attend the services. The provisions for the table were supplied in answer to prayer. Flour, vegetables, meat, and money came in abundance, and they lacked no good thing; and hundreds were fed who came as visitors and guests. They always knelt in prayer before eating, and with songs and praises partook of what God provided. 'Heaven came down their souls to greet, and glory crowned the mercy-seat.' A pipe from the city water works came right into the eating hall, which was very convenient. Seventy-five dollars was paid for the use of the grounds.

"About three weeks were consumed by the meetings, including the days spent in preparation and clearing up. It lasted over three Sabbaths. We were privileged to be there five days of this time. The meeting grew in interest and depth of earnestness from the beginning to the end. The altar work was of the most thorough stamp of anything it had ever been our privilege to see. Lost souls were never left alone. Sometimes the altar work did not close till near morning and seekers nearly always came through before they left the altar. There was no daubing with untempered mortar by those engaged in the meeting direct.

"The singing was the best we ever heard. The words and music both were largely composed by the singers themselves. So they were prepared under the inspiration of the Spirit for all stages of Christian experience. Wherever a seeker needed help, help was ready.

"The young people who had given their lives to this work showed remarkable adaptation for everything that seemed to be required of them. They were as ready to do drudgery as anything else. Order was excellent, considering the crowds that assembled every night—from one thousand to three thousand.

"One thing was noticeable and that was the almost entire freedom from anything of a self-nature. Very little was said of anything but salvation. To get an opportunity to testify, one had to be ready, stand up and hold his place until his turn came. There was no time to waste. There was seldom any preaching in the morning, as the love-feast nearly always ran until dinner time before the order of the meeting could be changed.

"There were representatives of nearly all denominations at this meeting. They came from far and near, but the bulk of those attending were from the Free Methodist church, as this work is a child of Free Methodism. There were campers from Canada, New York, Pennsylvania, Ohio, Illinois, Michigan, Iowa, Missouri, Kansas, Wisconsin, Texas, and Indiana, whom we met. How many more states were represented it is hard to tell. It was indeed a national camp-meeting.

"A great many came to see what they had heard a great deal about. Some came with hearts full of prejudice and misgivings in regard to the work of the Pentecost Bands. Others came to get saved and die the death to carnality. It was a melting time. Hearts were united as never before. Eternity alone will unfold the amount of good done in this meeting. Others came to learn more of the work. The spirit of heaven, which is harmony and love, was manifest on every hand. Walls of prejudice came tumbling down. Misunderstandings were corrected. Mutual acknowledgments were made and the Spirit of Christ ruled the grounds.

"The following ministers were present: J. W. Dake, Iowa; T. J. Noland, W. B. M. Colt, and F. D. Brooke, Illinois. These were acting chairmen in their respective conferences. Benson H. Roberts, principal of Chili Seminary; T. J. Gates, evangelist. Pastors and preachers, G. W. Griffith, I. J. Brown, T. B. Adams, J. N. Eason, W. S. Sansom, D. W. Sala, M. N. Huston, J. M. Turgeson, Brother Hull, J. S. Robinson, Father Tinkham, I. J. Langdon. Besides these there were others whose names we did not get. These were all outside of the Band work.

"There were several marked features about the camp-meeting which made it approach the nearest to the apostles' line of any we ever attended. First, the unbounded hospitality exercised. Mr. Dake literally obeyed the command, 'Use hospitality one toward another without grudging.'"

"This hospitality brought many to the camp-meeting who could not take care of themselves, who would have been deprived of the benefits and blessings but for it. Mr. Dake trusted in God to supply the needed provisions to feed all who should come. God honored his faith. From seventy-five to a hundred were fed at a meal, and never did they fare so well. From all quarters help came. Potatoes, apples, flour and fruit were shipped in liberal quantities from various points in Illinois, Michigan and other states. Money also was sent from friends of the work. It was an interesting scene, as the workers and visitors gathered in the long dining hall at meal time.

"The second feature was the unity of the Spirit which prevailed all over the camp ground. There was no discord, no clashing, no sulking; all was free and harmonious.

"Third, was the remarkable missionary spirit which prevailed. This was so great that it might be called a missionary camp-meeting. There was scarcely a service in which the Spirit did not lead out on the line of missions, and it was wonderful how God set His seal to this line of work. Some special missionary meetings were held, the first being devoted to the interest of the India mission, and as the two sisters and others spoke the Lord manifested His approval by showers of blessing until at times it was glorious. The England Band had its special meeting, where God again manifested His approval in repeated blessings. Although so many hearts were drawn out for the dark regions beyond the sea, it did not in the least detract from the work of soul-saving at hand, but rather seemed to further it, for the tide of salvation ran high from the beginning of the meeting.

"Many souls were saved and reclaimed, and a goodly number obtained the experience of holiness. Lastly, were the glorious manifestations of divine approval in various ways. Sometimes the glory would fall in an indescribable manner, and again there would be such a sense of God's presence as filled many souls with silent awe. One Saturday forenoon was this especially the case, as the Spirit led out on missionary work and other lines of truth. Some were overpowered and sank down, others fell on their faces, and all recognized the glorious presence of the great God."

On the last Sabbath afternoon, the Bands formed in

line according to their numbers with Mr. Dake at their head. Converts and friends joined the company until the ground was nearly encircled with a line of triumphant, singing soldiers of the cross. A very large ring was formed, and with crowds of people surrounding it this meeting took the form of a farewell service for the outgoing Bands. It was a glorious hour. The windows of heaven were opened and showers of blessing fell. Many hearts were moved by the triumphant testimonies and shining faces of those "who counted not their lives dear unto them." Preceding this farewell march and meeting, memorial services were held in the large tabernacle for those who had died during the past year, three on foreign fields and two on the home field. This was a tender, yet triumphant service. There was nothing somber about it. Instead of the black garb of mourning so commonly worn for the dead, the greater part of the sisters wore white dresses, the emblem of purity and heaven. There were some tears as several spoke of the dead and their labors.

Mr. Dake spoke last. His words, which seemed prophetic of his coming death, will be interesting, and we insert some of them as taken down at the time: "Five have gone to glory from our ranks this year, three from Africa and two from the home fields. We feel far less sorry over these than over those who ran from the field. I do not wish them back. I see a heavenly band around the throne. They are joining in the song of Moses and the Lamb. Thank God for this hour and for this inspiration. Next Harvest Home, if Brother Dake's place should be vacant, let there be no tears, but let clear testimonies, happy faces, and white dresses tell of triumph, for I shall surely join the band around the throne." He little thought —nor did any one—that his place would be vacant at the next annual Harvest Home.

CHAPTER III

THE TRIP TO GERMANY

Being much worn in body and in need of rest, Mr. Dake, through the kindness of friends, accepted an invitation to accompany them to Germany. They started May 1st, 1889. Under this date he writes:

"God has wonderfully opened my way. Brother Hofert, of Chicago, pays all my expenses. I have much to praise God for. We started by the Grand Trunk railway for New York City."

"May 4th. This morning we boarded the steamship *Veendam* of the Royal Netherlands line, bound for Rotterdam, Holland. We passed through the harbor by the magnificent figure of the Goddess of Liberty, and out into the Atlantic ocean. Often I have read of the ocean and seen its outlines on the map, but now for the first time I am lost in its immensity. What a masterpiece of God's handiwork, reminding me of the great God whom I serve, —too deep, too wide to be comprehended by my littleness. How I feel my humanity as I look on the grandeur of its singing waves. O Jesus! I love Thee more and more! This is my first day at sea. Sisters Haberlien and Hofert, of Chicago, are also on board, going to visit friends in Germany."

"May 5th. This is the Sabbath. I am holding prayers twice and three times a day with the steerage passengers, and this evening I preached to them a while and had good attention. I am holding up Jesus, and His light is on my soul. We are having very pleasant weather."

"May 6th. Every day we see steamships. One is now far away on our southern quarter. Have had some opportunity to speak for the Lord to-day. I have been thinking and praying much for my dear wife. May God anoint her with power from on high and give her many souls. I have the assurance that I will have success on my journey. We had prayers twice to-day in the steerage. In the evening the passengers played cards and swore and talked loud while I prayed, but God was with me and gave me great grace and patience, so I loved them all."

"May 7th. Still the weather is fine. We saw a steamship in the morning and asked her to report us at New York. God has made those ashamed who acted so rudely while at prayers and they are very kind and were present at prayers twice to-day. Glory to God! Oh, how good He is!"

"May 9th. The sea is rough to-day. The waves roll high. Saw a school of porpoises. They leaped clear out of the water in their gambols. Many of the passengers are sick. The Lord graciously gives me good health and favor with the passengers."

"May 10th. Arose at four a. m. Went out on the stern of the ship and spent an hour alone with Jesus. Oh, such a precious hour. I got such a hold of God for the success of my mission to Germany; also was much led out in prayer for my wife that she should find the place of responsibility which she ought to fill in the work of the Lord. O Jesus, I thank Thee for that precious hour, one of the sweetest of my life. I have had a blessed morning.

"Saw a whale for the first time. He arose out of the water ten or fifteen feet, three or four times. I am among a drinking, swearing, gambling set, but my soul is kept in perfect peace. The waves are rolling quite high, so that the tossing of the ship is breaking the dishes in the pantry. We had a rough time at prayers to-night. Some card players grew very boisterous while we prayed, and continued to laugh and curse and yell after we retired until two a. m., but the Lord kept me sweet."

"May 11th. Ship rocks considerable. Arose at five a. m., and went to prayer. God is with me. All around me is drinking, gambling, swearing, etc., but my soul is separated from sinners. Had a hard time at prayers to-night because of mockers."

"Sabbath, May 12th. I have kept this day unto the Lord. Held prayers with the passengers twice; otherwise there has been no indication of the Sabbath on board the ship."

"May 13th. We are drawing near the English coast and are looking for the lighthouse on Scilly Island. Expect to be in sight of 'Merrie England' to-morrow. In the last twenty-four hours we have come two hundred and eighty-five miles."

"May 14th. This morning for the first time in ten days we saw land. How good it seems to see it. I am so thankful to God who has brought me safely through to the present hour. After passing the Lizard, we saw the rocky coast of Cornwall, England. Beautiful fields are in sight, dotted with houses, castles, forts, lighthouses, signal stations, etc. We have not yet sighted France. We have passed the Island of Portland, with its citadel and frowning battlements. I long to be in England and fight a battle for the Lord. About seven p. m. we passed the Isle of Wight with its many historical connections."

"May 16th. We steamed up the Rhine to Rotterdam. We passed Delhaven, from whence the Mayflower started on its journey two hundred years ago. Holland is a pretty land. Long-armed windmills are seen everywhere. The houses are mostly tiled. I went ashore at Rotterdam. The streets are very clean, even the alleys being paved. One sees many strange things. Most of the draying is done by carts, drawn or pushed by men, with a dog or two hitched up to help.

"I accompanied Sisters Hofert and Haberlien to the train, which they boarded for Colmar. Then I took the train for Amsterdam, passing through The Hague, the capital, and Leyden, the most ancient city of Holland, also Harlaam. Here I am alone among the Dutch in Amsterdam.

"I took a room at a hotel, and after I had rested I boarded the tram car and had a view of the city. It is built on canals. Many of the streets are narrow but well-paved. In the evening I went to the Crystal Palace, a wonderful building. I am the Lord's, soul and body."

"May 17th. I awoke late this morning. Went to Ryke's Museum, comprising two hundred rooms full of paintings. The greatest works of the Dutch masters are here—Vandyke, Rembrandt, and others. 'The Descent from the Cross' was fine. 'Joseph Fleeing from Potiphar's Wife' was very striking. The dam is a public place around which are the palace and other buildings.

"I am sitting in a little shop where I have just had some chocolate, milk and biscuit for dinner, the first I have eaten to-day. I am not alone in this strange land, for God is with me. The streets are very crooked, but the canals are straight. People come to market on the canals. The tram cars are similar to our American street cars.

"From Amsterdam I came to The Hague, the national capital. I went about the city some. Visited the Houses of Parliament and the old prison gateway where prisoners were confined in the times of the Spanish inquisition. These buildings were erected in the fifteenth century. I also visited the Protestant cathedral of the fifteenth century, and went through the palace. It is plainly yet richly furnished. I saw some magnificent presents which were given to the king on his silver wedding. One of them was a table, costing £4,000 or $20,000. From The Hague I came again to Rotterdam at the request of the missionary of the Seamen's Home. I had a blessed time at family prayers. I must note the fact that the fields in Holland are flat and ditches run at short distances. The Hollanders are a very polite people, young and old touch their hats to strangers. Would that Americans were thus courteous. But a more slow-going race than these Hollanders is hard to find. They go to market on canal boats which they push along with poles, or else raise a small sail if the wind is favorable. I am pleased with the country."

"May 18th. This morning I took a steamboat for a trip up the Rhine. There are villages all along the river. We have just passed two frowning forts, one on each side of the river, which is full of all kinds of crafts, large and small, steam and sail. Church spires, towers and domes meet one's eyes in nearly every direction.

"Yesterday at The Hague when I reached the depot, the guide ordered a cup of milk for me, and I supposed a cup of coffee for himself; but his coffee proved to be beer. I told the waiter to take it away, as I did not drink beer myself, nor could I pay for it for some one else. They seemed much astonished, but the beer was removed.

"Praise the Lord! I have a sweet sense of His presence. I expect to stop at Emmerich on the border of Germany over Sunday and proclaim Jesus to the people. I have been on the boat for two days. I must leave her tonight, as I have never traveled on the Sabbath when it was avoidable, and although I must stop among strangers with but little money in my pocket, I will trust God."

"May 19th. The holy Sabbath finds me in Emmerich. After the morning meeting at the Evangelical Lutheran church I visited the Catholic cathedral. This is an ancient building. I was told that the body of the church was built in the fifth century, and the spire in the thirteenth century. It is at one corner of the town and is enclosed by walls, which were formerly walls of defense for the city.

"In the afternoon I took my Bible and went out into the country. I walked down the Rhine until I came to a quiet place, then I had a good talk with my Lord, and the peace of heaven like a benediction settled down on my soul. While I was praying a German came along and asked, 'Are you sick?' I told him, 'Oh, no, I am praying; that is all.' "

"May 20th. I again resumed my journey up the Rhine. It is now two a. m. here, and while I am writing this the brethren and workers in Michigan and Illinois and my dear wife in Iowa are doubtless engaged in their Sabbath evening services, as it is about 8 p. m. there.

"The view from the river is beautiful. An old ruin of the fourteenth century, the residence of the king, stands on the left. It is called Kaiser swert. Dasseldorf is a large tower with an old ruin castle on the river bank. The castle or fort was built in the sixteenth century. Landing at Cologne I visited the great cathedral, which was the most conspicuous object in sight. It is called the greatest Gothic church in the world. It was commenced in 1248 and consecrated in 1322 and has been completed only within a short time. It is 444 feet long, 201 feet wide externally and 282 feet through the transcepts. The height of the roof inside is 145 feet, the height of the spires 512 feet.

"It is wonderful to walk beside it, but to enter and see its vast yet architectural proportions, and its beautiful finish is grand indeed. In the south aisle are the windows presented by Louis of Bavaria in 1846. I ascended five hundred and two steps on the main spire. From there I had an excellent view of the city and surrounding country, the beautiful Rhine valley with its cities and villages, and Cologne with its many churches.

"I visited St. Andrews church, which contains the body of Albertus Magnus; also the church of St. Ursula, reputed to contain the bones of the eleven thousand virgins who were slain by the Huns, but they could not be seen. I also visited the church of St. Gereon, built in memory of the Theban legion and their captains, Gereon and Gregory, who suffered martyrdom in the reign of Diocletian. I saw the skulls of many martyrs set in the walls. We left Cologne at half past nine p. m."

"May 21st. I arose this morning at half past one in time to see Castle Crag of Drachensfels. It is 1,066 feet high. The castle was built in the twelfth century. Esperlia, farther down, is a basaltic cliff, 665 feet high. We passed Lintz on the left hand as you go up the river. It is an ancient walled town. Andernach on the right is one of the most interesting towns on the Rhine. Its ruined castle, lofty watch tower and ancient walls were in plain sight from the ship's deck. The tower has a breach made by the French guns in 1688. At Neowidon on the left, I saw the German palace of the Prince of Wales. It is a large, oblong building, situated close to the river, and of plain though pleasant architecture. Across the river from Neowidon is Weissenthurne, and on a hill back of the town I could see the monument to the French general, Hoche, who crossed the river here in 1797.

"Engers on the left is where Cæsar is supposed to have crossed the Rhine the second time. We passed the island of Niederwirth, and saw its prettily cultivated fields and convent church built about 1500 A. D. Coblentz is at the junction of the Rhine and the Moselle and is quite a large town. Right opposite is the Gibraltar of the Rhine, Ehrenbralzur. It is the strongest fortress in Germany, a high and rocky crag, fortified and casemated from bottom to top. The rocks are also perforated with subterranean works. The castle of Stolzenfels belongs to Queen Augusta, and is one of her summer residences. It is on the side of a little hill three hundred feet above the Rhine. It was first built in the thirteenth century, destroyed by the French in the seventeenth, and now restored.

"Across the river is Oberlahinstein, and just above it is

the pretty old castle of Lahnech. It has a legend con-
nected with it as all the old castles have. Rhense on the
right has a wall of the fourteenth century. Ranbrach on
the left is overtopped by the superb setting of Marksburg
castle. This is the boldest, most romantic spot we have
yet seen on the Rhine. The castle sits on the summit of
this rocky crag like a king on a throne. Above Bornhofen
are the twin castles of Steinberg and Libershien. They
are close together on two rocky peaks. The vineyards ex-
tend to the very foundations of the castle.

"We are in the midst of the famous Rhenish vineyards.
The mighty hills which here hem in the river on both sides
are almost covered with vines. All up the slope amid sec-
tions of rocks and boulders are the vineyards. This is
the most beautiful scenery I have ever seen. The hills
are from two hundred to a thousand feet high and enclose
us completely. All the way from Coblentz the scenery
grows more intensely wild and picturesque. Villages,
towns, cities, citadels, towers and castles pass by in quick
succession. A railroad runs on each bank of the river,
close to the water's brink. Just here on the right the
hills are so rocky that no vineyards can be planted.

"Oh, the grandeur of this unsurpassed scenery! It
speaks volumes of praise to Him whose I am and whom I
serve. Far above Welmich is seen the castle of Thurnberg,
or the Mouse, built in the fourteenth century. It is a
gloomy, grand old pile of ruins. The legend that gave it
the name of Mouse, is that an oppressor of the poor was
there eaten by mice. Over four hundred years since its
construction, and where are its gay occupants? Who were
they? Where are they buried? Thus in ruin and oblivion
ends all earthly grandeur.

"I saw the ruins of Castle Rheenfels, the largest pile
I have yet seen. Its situation is not so commanding as
Marksburg, but the castle pile is wonderful. From the
bottom of the hill to the top it was wall after wall. On

the left above the town of St. Goarhauser, is the castle of the Cat. St. Goarhauser lies across the river. Zurlei is an immense rock four hundred and thirty-three feet high. The river makes a sharp turn around the rock. At this place the railroads on each bank run through tunnels. The right hand road requires two tunnels to enable it to evade this rocky river pass. We have just come in sight of Oberwesli. It has a Gothic church of the fourteenth century, but the tower has never been finished. Several old towers lend a picturesque appearance to the place. The castle of Shonberg erected in the twelfth century is also in plain view. The hills slope back from the town, while across the river they arise almost perpendicular from the water. The old wall of the tower is quite well preserved.

"Caub on the left comes next, and above it the castle of Sutenfels. In the river in front of the town is 'The Plattz,' built by Louis of Bavaria, in the fourteenth century to exact toll from the vessels passing in the river. It is queerly built, rising one story high, with port holes and projecting windows, and a smaller tower rises from the center.

"The scenery here is beautiful. The hills are a perfect network of vineyards, while the town is built in a line along the base of the hills with 'Plattz' in front and the castle in the rear ground. Now I see the old ruins of Stohleck and Farstenberg, two castles close together. On the left, Torch has a church built in the thirteenth century. It is in a remarkable state of preservation. Across the river on the left is Neederhelmbeck, and above it the castle of Heimburg. And then in succession the castles of Loonceh, Fahlenberg, and Rheinstein. The last two have been restored and present a very correct appearance of a feudal castle.

"And now comes to view 'Sweet Bingen on the Rhine.' Oft I have read of it, but little dreamed that I should behold it, but it is even so. We behold and are now draw-

ing toward Bingen, which has existed in story and song.
And it certainly deserves the appellation of 'Sweet Bingen
on the Rhine.' It is at the juncture of the Rhine and Nake.
The town is situated in the basin formed by the junction
of the rivers. Opposite, on the wooded height of Neider-
wald, is the national monument commemorating the resto-
ration of the German Empire. It stands seven hundred
and forty feet above the river and consists of a pedestal
seventy-eight feet high. The town extends to the banks of
the two rivers and off on the slopes of the lofty hills at
the rear.

"We stayed in Bingen only a few minutes, and now
we are steaming for Mayence. It is more level here. For
the first time in traveling many long miles I can see away
into the country. We came to Mayence at three p. m. I
went to see the church, a fine old structure of the tenth
century, but it was not open and, being very weary, I did
not go farther. Mayence was a Roman camp, B. C. 38.
We remain here until three a. m., when we start on our
last day's journey."

"May 22nd. I left the ship this morning at Worms,
and now I am on the very spot where Luther met and
defied the pope and the prelates. Emotions profound fill
my heart, and tears fill my eyes, as I think of that little
monk standing here on that eventful day. He saw arrayed
against him the temporal and ecclesiastical powers, with
the pope at their head, and intent on his destruction. Yet
hear him say: 'Here I stand, I can not do otherwise. God
help me.' He depended on God in that awful hour and
refused to compromise his principles.

"Where the Diet of Worms was held is now a mansion
surrounded by a beautiful garden, in which I am penning
these notes. Close at hand is the great cathedral, built in
the thirteenth century. It is a silent morning hour, much
different from the time when Luther was confronted by
his bitterest enemies and took his stand by the grand

truth, 'The just shall live by faith.' That stand and that truth shook the foundations of Rome and gave us the Reformation.

"I was much impressed with a view of Luther's monument. It stands on a square substructure and measures forty-one feet, nine inches on each side. At the four corners are pedestals of polished syenite, eight feet, two and three-fourth inches high, on which are the statues of the mightiest supporters and promoters of the Reformation, Frederick the Wise, Elector of Saxony, nine feet in height; Philip the Magnanimous, Landgrave of Herse, nine feet, two inches; Philip Melancthon, nine feet, ten inches; John Reuchlin, nine feet, one inch.

"In the inner area sits a female figure emblematic of the cities of Augsburg, Magdeburg and Speyer. On the inner faces of the battlements are the arms of the twenty-four cities which fought and suffered for the Reformation. On the four socce pillars jutting out from the richly ornamented chief pedestal are seated the statues of the four earliest champions of the Reformation, viz.: The Frenchman, Peter Waldrus, 1187; the Enlishman, John Wycliffe, 1397; the Bohemian, John Huss, 1425; the Italian, Hieronymus Savonarola, 1498. These are surmounted by the colossal statue of Luther, eleven feet, four inches high, with a pedestal twenty-eight feet towering above and crowning the whole. In front we read the bold, decisive words, which were perhaps the indirect cause of the monument being erected: 'Here I stand, I can not do otherwise! God help me! Amen.' Many of Luther's energetic expressions and engravings of incidents in his life relative to the Reformation are to be seen in different places about the monument.

"The women of the town come to the bank of the river to wash their clothes. There were scores of them washing in the river and spreading their clothes on the grass, or hanging them on lines to dry. I sat on the entrance to the ferry across the Rhine and ate my bread and orange, and drank milk from a beer bottle. I have been strangely moved while visiting Worms, and I vow to be true to God. I know the war will rage; but I am the Lord's alone and He will keep me.

"I came by train to Manheim, and am now waiting for a train to Colmar. An awful scene is before me. Every waiting-room in this country is a saloon and men and women are all drinking beer. My soul is burdened, but what can I do? Only pray and cry out against it."

The following interesting letters were written from Germany to Rev. B. T. Roberts and wife:

"Manheim on the Rhine, May 22.
"Dear Brother and Sister Roberts: I came here to-day. I spent the forenoon in Worms. I sat on the spot where Luther said, 'Here I stand. I can do no other. God help me! Amen.' What thrills went through me as I saw the little monk defying the whole power of Rome. Tears filled my eyes and I vowed anew to be true to God.

"The Luther monument in Lutherplatz is very fine. It represents Luther making his great declaration quoted above. In front, on the outer battlement and at his right and left, stand Frederick the Wise, Elector of Saxony, and Philip the Magnanimous, Landgrave of Hesse; at his back to his right and left, Philip Melancthon and John Rench-lin. Immediately about Luther and seated at his feet, are Peter Waldrus, John Wycliffe, John Huss and Hierony-mus Savonarola. On the outer battlement where the elector and the other three stand, and between them are three female figures, one representing Augsburg with a palm branch, Magdeburg lamenting her desolate homes, and Speyer protesting. The chief pedestal consists of three parts, the sides of polished syenite and the upper and under of bronze cube. The upper cube has on each face an energetic expression of Luther's and the medallion portraits of two reformers. There are portraits of John the Constant and Frederick the Magnanimous, Electors of Saxony; Ulric Hutten and Francis Sickingen, Justus Jonas and John Bugenhagen, John Calvin and Ulric Zwingli. The lower cube has scenes in his life. On one side Luther before the Diet of Worms; on another Luther nailing his Theses to the Cathedral gates at Wittenberg; on another Luther administering the communion in two kinds, and Luther's marriage; on another Luther translating the Bible and preaching. It was the work of seven different men, yet it would take a sharper eye than mine to observe any difference in the work. It is very fine. I enjoyed it much.

"The site of the Diet of Worms has been purchased by a Lutheran gentleman, who has converted it into a lovely garden, and has built a fine mansion called the Heylshe House.

"My boat stopped six and one-half hours at Cologne, so I had ample time to visit the great Cathedral. You can only know it to see it. It is beyond words to convey the feelings you have in looking at that grand piece of art. It is immense, and yet has been so gracefully executed, that you know not which to admire most, its sublimity or its beauty. Its proportions, no doubt, you know, 512 feet high, 444 feet long externally, 282 feet wide, and 145 feet high, inside. I ascended about 520 steps to get the magnificent view from the dome, and I am tired yet. I visited also the church of St. Gereon, dedicated to the Theban Legion and their captains, Gereon and Gregory, who were all martyrized during the persecutions of Domitian. There are many skulls, said to be theirs, worked into the walls.

"Oh, I can not tell you the beauty of the Rhine Valley! I got up at 1:30 a. m. and strained my eyes till we stopped at Bingen, at three in the afternoon. It was a succession of hills from 200 to 1,000 feet high, towns with old walls, and towers, and castles, frowning from almost every crag. I had looked the subject up and was well prepared to understand and enjoy it.

"But amid all this beauty the blight of sin is on this country. I am glad I am an American. I appreciate it more than I ever did. While I write in the waiting-room men and women are drinking beer. Beer flows constantly everywhere. It will need consecration to the death to accomplish anything in this land of beer and dancing. Pray for me. I am determined to live true to God.

"Duramelzen, May 24. I am at the end of my journey. I find a happy, saved people. Sixteen came the first night I was here, and I was able to read, pray and talk in German. We had a blessed time. There is the nucleus of a good work here. They want workers. They are well to do. Can you not have the General Rules translated into German and printed, also your articles, 'Two Wines,' and, 'Sacramental Wines'?"

"Durrenentzen, Germany, May 31.

"Dear Brother Roberts: You can scarcely have an idea of the depth of darkness there is in this land on the question of liquor drinking. I am in the great grape growing region. Vineyards are on every hand, luxuriant and prolific. There are about fifteen saved people here who really know God, and yet they make, drink and sell wine,—or had done so to the time of my coming here. With my imperfect German, but with my heart on fire, I have gone into the fight, and nearly all have quit drinking wine.

"But the great question is, what shall we do with our vineyards? There is no sale for grapes at all. They must remove their vineyards entirely. I do not know how many will stand the test. I have told them they could not make, drink nor sell wine among us. You should have heard the Bible arguments they brought up: the feast at

Cana in Galilee; Paul to Timothy; 'the Son of man came eating and drinking, and they say, Behold a winebibber, (this is a stronghold with them); the day of Pentecost. 'These men are filled with new wine' in the German Bible reads 'suzzen weins,' sweet wine. They fortify themselves here. But God has helped me. I wish we could have some of your good articles on wine translated into German, when it is imperative that we have the General Rules and Articles of Religion and questions to members translated. I shall organize as best I can without. I tell them what are in them.

"I expect to sail from Rotterdam, June 15. I have gone into Switzerland since my last writing. I visited the church at Basel, where Erasmus is buried; also the old church of the eleventh century at Zurich, where Ulrich Zwingli used to preach. It made me feel solemn as I trod the streets where these men used to walk, where to name Jesus Christ was as much as their lives were worth.

"I also saw the great Strassburg cathedral. It is very fine, but does not come up to the Cologne cathedral. The clock was all I had looked for. I was there at the hour of twelve, saw the twelve apostles march and heard the cock crow and flap his wings three times—all very natural."

"May 23rd. I arrived in Colmar at half past twelve a. m., but could not find an empty bed in the place, so I sat on the sidewalk and prayed and praised the Lord until morning. I was thankful it was not raining. I thought of Him who had not where to lay His head, and of Jacob's pillow of stone; and though I did not see the angels as did the patriarch, yet I felt their presence.

"I started for Durrenentzen this morning through a most charming country; passed several villages and reached my destination at seven p. m. I went at once to the house of John Hofert, the brother of my Chicago friend who has so nobly helped me on this trip, and whose excellent wife came over in the same ship. I find real saints among these hospitable Germans. Glory to Jesus! In the evening seventeen or eighteen gathered into the house and we had a blessed time. I prayed and sang and talked, though my German is somewhat defective."

"May 24th. This has been the most precious day I ever spent on earth. At four a. m., while singing and praying, my soul was much blest, my face was bathed in tears, and I got such a sight of Jesus on the cross as charmed my soul. I was much impressed with the words of Isaac Watts:

'When I survey the wondrous cross
    On which the Prince of glory died,
My richest gain I count but loss,
    And pour contempt on all my pride.'

I saw so plainly that no matter what I received, it was purchased by the blood of Calvary, and that excluded all human boasting."

"May 26th. I arose at four a. m., and had a blessed hour and a quarter's talk with my adorable Master. How I saw my own littleness. He showed me clearly that 'they that dwell in the secret place of the Most High shall abide under the shadow of the Almighty.' This afternoon the people gathered in from the surrounding villages and I read a chapter in German and preached from Mark 8: 34. God lifted me up much and gave power to His word. I felt God was fitting me. After speaking-meeting, we held an altar service and five came to the altar seeking holiness. God was there."

"May 28th. We took the train for Strassburg to-day and went at once to the great cathedral. It is a wonderful building, but not so striking as the one at Cologne. The clock is the greatest curiosity. I was there at noon and saw it in operation after eleven a. m. At the first quarter a child comes out and strikes the quarter; at the second quarter a youth comes out and strikes; at the third quarter a middle-aged man strikes; at the fourth, an old man. Thus all the stages are represented. Then death with a scythe in one hand strikes the hour of twelve. When he strikes, a child below turns the hour glass over. When the striking ceases, the twelve apostles pass out in front of the Savior, and each one bows to Him, and as they pass, the cock flaps his wings and crows three times.

"The clock keeps the Zodiac. All the planets move in their order, just as they move about the Zodiac, and with the same time. A ball representing the moon turns just as the moon is full or partial. A globe turns on its axis as the earth turns. A hand shows what hour the sun rises each day, another what hour it sets. The clock keeps the day of the month, also the ecclesiastical time. The room was crowded with people to see it.

"I ascended to the roof of the building, and had a beautiful view of the city. The church is Gothic and was begun 1015 A. D. Right near it stands the oldest dwelling-house in the city, six hundred years old. I saw also the monument of Gutenberg, inventor of the printing press. The war of 1871, between the French and Germans, raged around Strassburg. I saw great earthworks about the city. I came back to Colmar in the forenoon; got acquainted with the head assessor. He invited me to his home. I went and prayed with him. God was with me."

"May 29th. This morning I arose at half past three and took an early train for Basle. On arriving here I went to the old Munster church, where lie the bones of Erasmus. I saw his sepulcher, also that of Empress Anne of Hohenburg, wife of Emperor Rudolph I, of Hapsburg. Count Thurstein also is buried here. He was the Protector of the Chapter, and died in 1318. This church was commenced in 1356 A. D.

"From Basle I went to Zurich, scene of the labors of

Ulrich Zwingli. He was slain in the battle with the Catholic canons. I visited the old church where he aroused
the Swiss to battle for their release from popery. It is
of the tenth century and very plain. I traveled nearly all
day amid charming Swiss scenery. What I have seen of
Switzerland is picturesque indeed. Took train back to
Mansenheim this evening and am again at Durrenentzen."

"June 2nd. This has been a glorious day. This afternoon I organized the First Free Methodist church (class)
ever organized on European soil. It numbered twelve.
They are all blessed, plain pilgrims. It has been a great
step for them, as they have had to give up their wine-mak-
ing, and this is the staple here. In the evening Brother
Haberlien, who lives in another village, took me and some
of the class over to his home, where I preached again. It
was a Catholic village, and a mob quickly gathered outside. They sang, yelled and swore, and then fell to fight-
ing. One man was stabbed."

"June 3rd. We walked to a village three miles distant
and held a meeting. One woman was at the altar seeking
the Lord, and many others wept loudly. There was much
conviction on them."

"June 4th. Good meeting to-night at Brother O's. The
whole class were seeking holiness."

"June 5th. In my morning devotions I was much impressed with the coming of the Lord. I must watch for
His coming. I see the great harvest, and so few to enter
in. Help, O Lord, and send laborers into Thy harvest field!
A little while and the kingdoms of this world must become
the kingdoms of the Lord and of His Christ. Every land
must hear the glorious news. God help me to forget every
earthly pleasure, to know no man after the flesh, and love
most where I see most of the image of Jesus, my Lord.
When I fall, I want it to be face foremost toward my purchased possessions. Glory to Jesus!

"I held to-day the first society meeting ever held in

Germany. We elected Brother H. class-leader. I did feel thankful to my prayer-answering God. I still feel much impressed about my Lord's coming. While praying in a barn God came with much inspiration to my soul."

"June 9th. A glorious Sabbath. Two more joined the class and the power of God was felt all day."

"June 10th. This morning I bade the friends good-by and started for Paris, France."

"June 11th. After traveling over French soil all night, this morning we came through beautiful country and are now in Paris before noon. We took a cab and went to Sister Hofert's uncle's, who is a servant of the Grand Duke. We found him in the Duke's palace. He took us to a restaurant for dinner. Then we went to the University Exposition,—I suppose the most wonderful one the world ever saw. I went upon the Eiffel Tower. It is a thousand feet high, and presents a grand view of the city. I have a nice boarding place here with a Swiss lady."

"June 12th. This morning we visited the 'Place De La Concordi,' saw 'Cleopatra's Needle' and the place where the guillotine stood where Louis XVI, Marie Antoinette, and three thousand others suffered death between June 21st., 1793, and May 3rd., 1795. I felt the solemnity of this place. We next visited the 'Arch De Triumph,' a magnificent piece of architecture. Then we passed on to the Madalian church. After dinner we went to the Hotel des Invalides, where the tomb of Napoleon is situated. It is one of the most beautiful things I have yet seen. As I stood and looked on the sarcophagus that contains all that is earthly of the mighty warrior, and thought of his battles and downfall and probabilities for another world, I was choked with emotion, and amid my tears I said:

'I'd rather be the least of them
    Who are the Lord's alone,
Than wear a royal diadem
    And sit upon a throne.'

"The tombs of Louis Napoleon and Joseph Napoleon and Marshalls Duroc and Bertram are also here. The beauties of the building and the rich furnishing can be understood only by being seen. Many of Napoleon's cannon are about the grounds.

"Next we went to the Palace of the Louvre and Tuileries. This kept us most of the afternoon. Hundreds of rare paintings and rich treasures of art are here. From this place we visited the Place De La Bastile. Here stood the old prison in which Madam Guyon was incarcerated. Thousands of others here suffered untold agony and a fearful death. It was destroyed in 1789."

"June 14th. Farewell to Paris—I am homeward bound. We leave the city of society to-day, and I rejoice at the thought of soon being again in the front ranks of the Lord's army. We had a pleasant ride through France, then crossed the line into Belgium. We passed close by the battle-field of Waterloo, and through Brussels, the capital. We also passed Antwerp, of historic fame. It is completely surrounded by earthworks. We arrived at Rotterdam at six p. m., and went on board the vessel."

"June 15th. At three a. m. we left Rotterdam and are now in the English Channel. I have been praying all the morning and feel much of the sweet peace of God in my heart."

"June 21st. To-day the camp-meeting begins at Ray, Indiana. The quarterly conference and the Michigan Bands have united to hold it. Brother A. Bradfield and Brother Nelson have it in charge. I am praying that God may make it a wonderful meeting. The wind increased all day, and at times the waves rolled over the upper decks. I was on deck much of the time and enjoyed the glorious scene."

"June 22nd. I have been much blessed to-day in praying God to send floods of holy rain on the camp ground at Ray, Indiana."

"June 27th. We reached New York at five p. m. Praise the Lord for the safe voyage! Left at nine p. m. for Chicago, Illinois."

"June 29th. I reached the camp ground at Ray, Indiana, two days before the meeting closed. God is here in power. Glory to His name! I was much helped in preaching in the evening. It seemed good to be in meetings again with the workers. The Lord gave us a time of blessing."

"June 30th. This has been the best Sabbath of my life. A time of power on the camp ground. Some preachers as well as others are seeking holiness."

"July 1st. The camp-meeting closed. The Lord gave us money to pay car-fares for ten workers to the annual Harvest Home to be held at Carlinville, Illinois. Brothers Shumway and Donley have again helped us nobly on finances."

"July 3rd. Reached Chicago to-day and spent the night at the hospitable home of Brother and Sister Hofert."

"July 4th. Brother Hofert's folks, Brother Harry Agnew, from Africa, ten workers and myself spent the day pleasantly in Lincoln park, and thanked God for the rest we enjoyed."

CHAPTER IV

REVISITS SCENES OF SCHOOL LIFE

Both time and space forbid us giving the details of the three years that intervened between Mr. Dake's return from Germany and his departure for Africa, but if possible they were filled with greater effort and more incessant toil than ever before. A short time before he left for Africa he desired to visit Brother and Sister Roberts at Chili, his spiritual birthplace and a spot ever dear to him. He recorded it thus:

"March 4th, 1891. Wife and I spent a number of days on this old battle-field. At Rochester, North Chili, Tonawanda, and Lockport, we were warmly welcomed and saw the hand of God in convicting and helping the people. The truth was gladly received. There are saints in this conference who know no retreat. There is a revolution taking place here. Young men, who believe in the Holy Ghost and who keep the unction on them, are coming to the front. A number of good revivals have been held in various parts of the conference."

After speaking of the needs at some places, he mentions the worldly conformity in dress and in house furnishings and says: "Here you see many finely furnished houses. Extravagance in furniture is at the expense of God's poor. Brussels carpet, silk, upholstered furniture, gilt picture frames, lace curtains, marble top furniture, etc., consume the money that might be used in pulling sinners out of the fire. God help us to keep to the plain way. It was in this conference I was converted, educated, and called to preach, and many old friends gave me a warm clasp of the hand and encouraged me in trying to 'girdle the globe with salvation.' "

He also reported a day at North Chili, which shows his own enjoyment of being among the friends of his school days and how he turned everything to God's glory and the helping of souls. We give it as he wrote it while there on this trip:

"Thursday, March 5th. Mrs. Dake and I came to the well-remembered place. Sister Benson Roberts met us at the depot and we were soon at the old farmhouse. On the way, we paused by the ruins of the old seminary, which had been burned down, and I pointed out to my wife the place where I was converted. It was a desolate scene— the crumbling fragments of the wall; but all are striving in faith and reaching forth to see it rebuilt (This has since been done).

"We were warmly and heartily entertained. God came to the evening meeting in power and two were blest. Father and Mother Roberts were present and in the Spirit. We stopped for the night at Professor Roberts'. The next morning we went to Father Roberts' to dinner in company with Benson and wife. We had just finished our dinner when a delegation of students arrived and filed into the house. They had learned that Mrs. Dake and I were going away that day, and held an indignation meeting and had come to request us to stay over the Sabbath. Of this their 'spokes-woman' informed us. We were much affected and the Holy Spirit filled the place. We told them our appointments were out but we would return next week and we would pray now. So we went to our knees, and there was a breaking up time. Three of them were blest and saved. Glory to God! At three o'clock in the afternoon Professor Roberts turned the school session into a meeting. God came again. Two more struck through into liberty. Oh, it was so blessed. Father Roberts was in his element and rubbed his hands and said: 'Amen! Praise the Lord!' and sang snatches of old-fashioned songs. Mother Roberts was plain and simple as ever. God endorsed the meeting. It made us think of old times when Albert Stilwell, Phil. Hanna, Emma Chesbrough, I myself and others were converted, and when Ida Winget, Jennie Sellew and Lucy Coleman, and Orlo Moore, now in heaven, used to shout for joy.

"There are plain pilgrims here now, but some have too stylish an appearance and some show compromise in their own dress and that of their children. But the truth was gladly received—more eagerly in fact than we have seen in any other place on our journey and the outlook is for a deluge of old-fashioned power. Professor and Mrs. Roberts promise God and the people that they shall have here a salvation school on Holy Ghost lines."

From his journal we quote the following:

"September 22nd. to 28th., 1891. Have been visiting the Bands and making preparation with a view to being absent several months in foreign lands. To-day I bade good-by to loved ones and started for Chicago, en route for New York."

"September 29th. Staid over night in Chicago. Wife is with me."

"October 1st. Bade wife good-by in Chicago to-day and started for New York."

Just before he sailed he sent the following parting words to the workers:

"DEAR FELLOW-REAPERS: In pursuit of our divine call to kindle watch-fires in every land, I embark October 7th., D. V., in the steamer *Majestic* of the White Star Line. Pray for me as I go to England, to Norway, Germany, and Monrovia to assist in making the watch-fires blaze. God is with us. We shall see the clean salvation exemplified in the lives of those who are now in darkness. My heart is with you in your toil and self-sacrifice. Do not lay the cross down. I know you will, if possible, be more true to God and souls while oceans roll between us than as though we were laboring together.

"Remember you are Free Methodists and keep the interest of the cause, which is dearer to you than life, always uppermost. No church contains such a proportion of fire-baptized saints, and we are joined to all the living. Oh, the wide-spread fields. See the towns all around you that need the light. See the men and women that pass you by the scores on their way to hell. Can not you stop them? Get them to pause for a moment, and say to them, 'BEHOLD THE LAMB OF GOD!' then look beyond the boundaries of the ocean at the millions in the blackness of the night of sin. Whose heart is shut against the ones for whom Christ dies? LOOK! LOOK! at the perishing multitudes hellward bound!

"Wanted! ten thousand to labor in every land. Wanted! those who will work without salary. Wanted! those who will take the fare by the way and shout, 'Glory to God!' Amen! They are coming; the tread of their feet is heard. There is a call from Jamaica, West Indies. Who will fill it? There are calls from Australia, Tasmania, and New Zealand. Who will go? Calls from Sweden and Germany wait for workers. Now, who wants to go home? Let all the faint-hearted pack their satchels and leave quickly to make room for the Gideons, the Shamgars, the Daniels, the Davids and the Deborahs, the Marys, the Pricillas, and the Dorcases, who are coming. Amen! All hail! With fingers in your ears, eyes on the mark, feet on the thorny path, hands filled with pitchers and lamps, hearts aflame, on to victory! Fellow-workers, I am with you on the battle-field and will be in the triumphal march."

CHAPTER V

THE MISSION TOUR TO AFRICA

"Sabbath morning, October 11th., dawned upon us and found us in the midst of the great ocean. We all desired that God should be glorified in that day. Three times I went to the steward before we obtained permission to hold an afternoon service. The steward said this was an Episcopal boat, etc., but finally he gave permission. The Rev. Mr. Nelson, of the United Methodist Free Church of England, assisted us. We sang, prayed and testified and I preached a short sermon from Luke 12:25. We had a good congregation and serious attention. We trust an impression was made for good. In the evening the Episcopalian minister officiated and told his hearers that all they had done on the boat in games and sports was to the glory of God, and he doubted not it was more to the glory of God than as though they had gone around praying and saying, hallelujah!

"While he was thus crucifying his blessed Lord in the saloon we were out on deck and a large crowd of steerage passengers were gathered on the lower deck and a number of cabin passengers on their deck. For an hour we sang glorious hymns and songs and testified, while the tide of blessing ran high. Amens came welling up and the melody of heaven went sweeping over the white-capped waves. It was the best hour I ever spent on the ocean. We told the steerage passengers that if we had been in charge of the boat we should have had them all in to divine service. They called out, 'Hear! Hear!' This is the English mode of applause.

"It was a grand time. Amen! Then we sang the dox-
ology and retired to roll and rock in our berths and sleep
the sleep of the just. We are all in good spirits. God's
service, the anticipation of coming conflict, and surety of
victory, cause us to rejoice in the Lord and joy in the God
of our salvation."

MESSAGES FROM ENGLAND

"Liverpool, England, October 19, 1891.
"MY OWN PRECIOUS WIFE:
"This is six a. m. I have been out to get some milk,
and Laura and Bessie have the toast and graham porridge
ready. Oh, such a day as I had yesterday. George and I
attended a mission kept by a man by the name of Herbert
Wood. He is an ex-member of the Church of England. He
calls his mission 'The Home of Love.' Then he has another
mission which is run by four ladies, 'The Slumworker's
Home.' George and I held a meeting at eleven a. m. Sabbath in 'The Home of Love.' Had a very good time. Only
converts and workers were present.

"In the afternoon we had an open-air meeting on the
steps of the slum home. Oh, what a sight! Little children, barefooted, dirty, ragged, with matted hair, pinched
and hungry-looking. Women filthy—faces as dirty as if
they had slept in a pigpen! Mamma, I never saw such a
sight. After the 'open-air' we invited them in. Some of
those poor, lost creatures came in. My heart broke! I
sobbed and cried and groaned, and the tears flowed in
streams from my eyes. Oh, mamma, I thought, could it be
possible they were made in the image of our lovely Jesus?
So lost!

"I threw myself anew recklessly out for a lost world,
and if you, Ida, had been here you would have given me
an extra push and said: 'Go, darling, go with all your

might, and my prayers shall be your wings.' Two poor women knelt at the altar, and my tears flowed for them. One of them was full of rum, but they both prayed. When the meeting was over two women stayed. I went and talked with them and they said they wanted a piece of bread. They had had nothing to eat that day. One was a poor, lost creature. The other was a Welsh girl of nineteen. She said her parents were dead. She had come to Liverpool to work, and after a time her work gave out. Then the woman where she boarded took her clothes. Then she could get no place because she lacked clothing. The night before she had slept in a four-cent lodging house! I am going to see what can be done for her. I hope to get her saved.

"Oh, God, have mercy on the lost of this awful city. I see your tears, my darling, and they flow as mine did over those for whom Christ died. Saturday I went out to Rochdale, where No. 15 are. Such a pretty ride through the green fields and quaint villages. I went down to Manchester, a great city where they make much of the cotton cloth of the world. At Rochdale I changed cars and went to Milnrow, two miles farther. I found them all of good cheer. It is a quaint old town with narrow streets and brick houses with slate roofs. I think the outlook for work is very good, blessed be God. My soul gets hotter and hotter. George and I start to-morrow for Norway, D. V. I have had a little sore throat, I guess because I have had no preaching to do, for since yesterday it is better. Glory to God! My soul exults and praises the Lord.

"I long to hear from you, and probably will in Norway. You will soon begin to get my letters, then you will hear from me often. Write me about everything. Love to all. Much love to yourself. Kiss the babies for me.

"Yours,   "V."

To the friends and workers in America he wrote an ac-

count of this meeting and heart-rending cases he saw, and
added:

"I said while in the midst of this awful scene, O Lord,
I'll run for Thee as I never have. O Pentecost workers!
prepare for an advance. You have only yet touched
the edge of the terrible layers of lost men. Some think
we work too hard, and sacrifice life and health too greatly.
But could you see these poor drunken wrecks who have
sacrificed body, soul and spirit to the devil, I think you
would say, no sacrifice is too great to rescue a lost world
from hell. While the many settle down in selfish ease, I
want to blow a trumpet so loud that you will all feel the
needs of the world and will rush forth to work and to
'COUNT NOT YOUR LIVES DEAR UNTO YOUR-
SELVES.'

"Right in this Liverpool slum work we want volunteers.
Who will arise and go? Pentecost workers, the whole
world needs the gospel we preach. Free Methodism in its
purity is what the world is dying for. Gird your loins
and get ready for the field God will send you to.

"Yours in the forefront,

"VIVIAN A. DAKE."

"Liverpool, England, 10-17-'91.
"MY DEAR MARY, CARRIE AND RUTH:
"Papa is well and blest and hopes and prays that you
may all be blest. The great Atlantic ocean, three thousand
miles wide, rolls between us, but Jesus is with us just the
same. I came over in a great ship as long as from our
front gate to the Rest Home. The great waves rocked it
like you rock your hammock; but God took care of us.
We are now in England.

"We landed at Liverpool, England. Get the atlas and
have mamma show you all the places that papa goes to.

You can see away across the ocean from New York City to Liverpool, on the map. Monday we go to Hull, on the other side of England. Then Brother Chapman and papa take the steamer to Bergen, Norway, and then another steamer to Sogndai, where Brother and Sister Ulness live. Yesterday papa went to see some wax men and women. There was Queen Victoria of England and her children, all life size; there were army generals and many others. A lady stood looking at the figures with a book in her hand. Brother Chapman thought she was alive, but when he looked closer he found that she was only wax· she was so life-like.

"There are many donkeys and Shetland ponies hitched to wagons five or six times as large as themselves. They call the street-cars, 'trams.' The trams have a place on the roof where people can ride. While papa was riding up there one day two little boys came running on the sidewalk and turning somersaults and going over on their hands and feet like a wheel. Then they would cry, 'Ha-penny, please.' A 'ha-penny' is a half-penny and equals one of our cents. The boys (one as large as Carrie) ran about a mile and then as we did not throw any half-pennies, they stopped running. Was that not a hard way to earn money? Think of those little boys on the street, going barefoot in the cold, and then think of your nice, warm home. Papa wants you all now to get down on your knees and sing 'Praise God, from whom all blessings flow', for your nice home. I expect you all to live for God. I pray much for you. God bless my darling children.

"As ever,

"PAPA DAKE."

"DEAR WIFE:

"Of course I have always thought that our girls would work in the Pentecost work, but this morning I have, under the pressure of the Spirit, consecrated Mary for India, Carrie for Africa, and 'Kittie' (Ruth) for any place He calls. Oh, oh! It brought the tears in showers, but I was glad to make the offering. Now then, if this be the will of God I shall praise Him forever! Be more careful with them in training them. They are the Lord's and we must be careful of another's property. Let Mary save her pennies; and talk to her about the missionaries and read to her about them from the papers. God bless you, my darling, and my sweet babies. "VIVIAN."

A SIDE TRIP TO NORWAY

"October 21st. From Hull, England, Brother Chapman and I took the steamer *El Dorado* to Bergen, Norway. We took steerage passage. It took us two days and two nights. We were able to endure it, but did not eat steerage fare. We had a very smooth voyage. We think our God smoothes the sea before us, as the steamers we have gone on, all the way from New York, have had very stormy voyages preceding the ones we took. On the steamer the chief engineer was very kind to us. He took us down and showed us all the new machinery of the boat and then took us into his cabin.

"We talked with him and asked the privilege of prayer. He knelt with us while we poured out our hearts to God. We believe it was not in vain. In the steerage we prayed constantly. A merchant of Aalesemend was with us. He was touched. When we landed at Bergen, he followed us to our boat (he was going another way) and bade us God-speed, and asked us several times to remember him in our prayers. He gave us a warm invitation to come to Aalesemend, Norway, and visit him. Thank God! We will have Brother Ulness go in our stead. So God helps us, as we travel, to sow the seed.

"We found the coast of Norway very beautiful. We changed steamers at Bergen, and took a coasting steamer. We saw beautiful scenery all the way. Villages at the foot of mountains hundreds of feet high. Cattle and sheep feeding on the sides of the mountains, and over beyond the higher snow-capped mountains four thousand feet above the level of the sea.

"After dinner to-day (October 23rd) Brother Chapman and I went into the steerage saloon and sang, read the Bible and prayed. We told the Lord that although the people could not understand us, yet He could make them feel the power of our prayers. When we finished, men, women and children were crowded all around us, looking on with interested faces.

"Inland we went on the bosom of the great fiords (ocean arms) until we came to Sostrand. There had been a dedication of an orphanage there and a great crowd came on the boat. They sang one of their songs, then Brother Chapman and I sang: 'I'm washed in the blood.' Then two schoolmasters spoke to us and asked us to please speak some 'good' to the people. We told them we could not talk Norwegian, but we could pray. So we prayed and God came. A great crowd gathered around. One of those who had spoken to us urged us to come to his village and thanked us very much. We shouted and praised God, and Brother Chapman had a time of blessing.

"We soon reached Sogndal. What a meeting with our dear Brother and Sister Ulness! We sank and wept and shouted. While the power fell, we sang, 'It is good to be here.' "

"Sogndal Norway, October 24, 1891.
"DARLING WIFE:

"Safe at last in Lillian's mountain home. Oh, it is so beautiful. I wish you were here. Out of the window I

can see an arm of the sea a mile wide. Sivert, George, and
I put a line out and caught a fish to-day. All around the
town are mountains two or three thousand feet high,
while one six thousand feet high shoves its snow-capped
summit up among the clouds.

"Away up the sides of the mountains you can see the
houses of the peasant farmers. The scenery is grand and
sublime. Sivert and Lillian were so glad to see us. We
sang, 'It is good to be here,' and God's power came on us
all. Bless the Lord! This afternoon we held a street meeting. A good many people came. I preached and Sivert
interpreted. We sang and prayed and gave God the glory.
Some wept and some were much stirred up.

"To-morrow we go away up the mountains to have
meeting. We have a street meeting in the afternoon and
meeting in a private house in the evening. God be with
you. Be true. Throw yourself out for souls. Do not stay
at home. Get out to meeting every Sabbath and at least
once a week. I did not hear from you here. We start
away from here Monday, November 2nd, D. V. Then I
shall look for mail from you at Milnrow. Write me in
Africa after November 1st. Love to all. I am so well
and free and blest. Glory to God! Tell the little girls
that papa loves them. Tell them papa went in a row boat
on the ocean to-day. It was very nice. We caught a fish
which we will have for dinner to-morrow. Wish you could
have some of our fresh fish. Pray much for me. It is now
six p. m., and is quite dark. It is half-past seven a. m. with
you. I shall retire for the night about the time you are
having dinner and prayers. Good-by.

"VIVIAN."

"October 24th. This is our first day at Sogndal. We
have been blessed all day. Have met some of the converts.
This afternoon we held an open-air meeting. Brother
Chapman and I talked and Brother Ulness interpreted for

us. Some were weeping, and we look for fruit. Sister
Ulness exhorted in very good Norwegian. We gave out a
meeting on the mountain for to-morrow morning, on the
street at two p. m., and in a private house in the evening.
The watch-fire is burning and we are doing our best to add
to the flame. Let all the friends of Norway pray. There
is a watch-fire here that will never go out.

"V. A. D."

In the following letter Mr. Dake further reports their
labors and victories during their brief stay in Sogndal:

"From the first our visit to Norway has been victorious.
The day after we arrived we held a street meeting and
every day since we have had two or three meetings a day.
On the Sabbath we held two street meetings, and in the
evening three came to the altar. Two of them belonged to
the middle class. They have been saved. Four have professed religion since we came. One of them is one of the
brightest saints I have seen. Her face shines with the
light from heaven. Pray for Madam I——, this blessedly
saved woman.

"There are now about fourteen who have been saved,
and the work is breaking out in new force and power. The
watch-fire has been much stirred up and is burning brightly. The Lutheran church stands right in the way, but our
God is mighty. To-day Brother and Sister Ulness had
their first money given to them that they have received
from Norway. It was sixteen krona and nine ore, equal
to four dollars and thirty-five cents. On Wednesday night
I made a call for a free-will offering for them, and Thursday forenoon two old men, one a rich miser, came down to
the house and gave them eight and one-half krona. This
was in direct answer to prayer. Sister Ulness had been
praying God to lay it on that man to give fifty kronas.
Oh, these ripening fields! How the fire burns! We are

seeing the best days of our life. God sent us to Norway, and results followed.   "V A. D."

"We left Sogndal, Norway, for Africa, via England, at one a. m. The parting was characteristic of this warm-hearted people. The converts sent us in food and little presents and shook hands with us over and over again. On the steamer we held meetings twice and God came in power. The passengers crowded around us. We are in the third-class saloon. Since we left England, Brother Chapman and I have traveled steerage. We stand it very well on these short trips; but for very long ones it is an unclean, unhealthful way of travel. By the time one has bought a bed and extra food, which all generally need, the expense is not much less than second cabin. In Bergen we staid until Monday, November 2nd. Here God helped us to kindle a fire that will not soon go out. Brother Chapman learned by inquiry that Rev. O. Eleson, a Methodist preacher and the father of a schoolmate of his, lived in Bergen. The young man, Joseph Oleson, had roomed with Brother Chapman two years at Evanston, Illinois.

"On Saturday evening we went to the first Methodist Episcopal church to hear Brother Oleson preach, and were surprised to find a bazaar going on. Brother Chapman met Brother Oleson and he asked him to speak. Brother Chapman got up, Brother Oleson interpreting, and told the people what Methodism was, and that worldly amusements were not needed to carry on the work. He talked plainly against their bazaars, etc. We stayed only a few minutes. What pain to find God's house turned into a 'house of merchandise.' In spite of this plain talk, the pastor came to me and asked me to preach for him Sabbath morning. We had four hundred to preach to. Brother Ulness interpreted for me and we had a time of blessing. Hot shots of truth pierced the hearts of the people. Sometimes they swayed to and fro and some stood on their feet and listened and many wept. There was a stir in the camp. Several came and asked us to stay a week and said we would have many souls.

"An old sea captain took me home to dinner with him, while Brothers Chapman and Ulness went with the janitor, who did not believe in the bazaar and rejoiced in the truth we had been preaching. At noon Brother Chapman gave the children a talk on Africa. At five p. m., Brother Chapman preached in the second Methodist Episcopal church, Brother Ulness interpreting. They had a great shout, both of them shouting the praises of God. About twenty came to the altar seeking holiness, among them our host at dinner, and some were much broken up."

RETURN TO ENGLAND

"By the blessing of God we came safely across the North Sea on the good steamship *Norge* and landed at New Castle-on-Tyne. The same night we ran up to Edinburgh, Scotland. We stood over the grave of John Knox, who said while wrestling in secret prayer, 'GIVE ME SCOTLAND OR I DIE.' We stood in the St. Giles cathedral where he preached. The Edinburgh castle was of melancholy interest as marking the place where many reformers and Covenanters met death.

"We stayed only a short time in Edinburgh and started toward London. We stopped at Sheffield. We found here a band of warm-hearted people. One brother had been formerly a Primitive local preacher, but on account of his out-spoken utterances on Bible holiness he had been forced to leave the Primitive church. He and his true-hearted wife were of one heart with us. We were given a home among them. We believe God has a band of pilgrims in Sheffield. They had never heard secret societies spoken against, but they agreed to the truth as

we spoke against them. Their gold rings they were willing to lay aside for Jesus. We had a blessed meeting with
them.

"From Sheffield, we came to Birmingham. On the
train we had a chance to speak to a young lady who promised to write us, and of whom we believe God will make a
worker. God was working on her heart. She was an
earnest, simple Scotch girl. At Birmingham we met a
man whose heart was all afire. He had joined the Salvation Army for the present. He praised God aloud that
we had come to England.

"We had by this time got about to the end of our money.
It was Saturday and we were going to London; we knew
no one there and must have money for lodging. We had
been in prayer and told the Lord all about our case. Just
as we were leaving brother T—s for the train he took out
his purse and gave us money enough to send us on our way
rejoicing. I said to him, 'How did you know that we had
but little money left?' He said he did not know, but God
told him to give. He entreated us to return to B., and
said God had a great work to do.

"We got into London after dark, and found a cheap
room up in the attic of a small hotel. We had a grand
time praying Saturday night, November 7th., until midnight for salvation among the Bands over Sabbath, and
felt that God answered." (This was his custom on Saturday evenings during the last months of his life.)

"Sabbath morning we went to service at Westminster
Abbey. In the afternoon we went to Wesley's Chapel,
City Road. Wesley laid the corner-stone April 1st, 1777.
He preached the dedication sermon November 1st, 1778.
Many times have these walls resounded with his voice.

"In the Bunhill Fields graveyard across the way we
saw the graves of John Bunyan, Susannah Wesley (mother
of John and Charles Wesley), and Isaac Watts. We were
much blest as we stood over the grave of Isaac Watts and

repeated his grand hymn, 'When I survey the wondrous cross,' etc. In Wesley's Chapel across the way we saw the demoralizing, blighting effect of worldliness. The church has been newly fitted up. They have prayer books, and in some things are not far behind the Established Church. They have the same high pulpit, the same tablets for the dead, and their house of resurrection which Wesley founded has indeed become a house of the dead.

"The service was a children's service. In the evening Brother Chapman attended the Salvation Army. Thus God is helping us. More and more I am convinced that in no land is there greater need of a church which preaches and holds to separation from the world than in England. We are here for that purpose and feel that God is opening our way before us. Hallelujah! My soul burns as we kindle watch-fires. I feel in divine order, and to God shall be all the glory.

"In England we found none that was with us on the line of separation from the world which we preach. I went to see Reader Harris, the leader of the Pentecost Mission Band. They teach and believe in holiness as a second work. They publish a paper called *Tongues of Fire*. I did not have time to find out whether they preached against secret societies and worldly doings in the church or not.

"We went to Smithsfields, where the martyrs were burned, and what a thrill it was to feel that they had 'loved not their lives unto the death.' Here Annie Askew was burned on the complaint of her husband. The noble John Rogers shouted the victory in the fire; also John Bradford and John Philpot. It was a grand place to my soul.

"The second day I was there we were holding an open-air meeting in front of a saloon. While I was praying some one threw a lot of water over us all. As the water came on us, the joy of the Holy Ghost fell also. What a blessed shout and victory we did have. When the water came the crowd fell back, for as is usually the case the devil wet his own soldiers worse than us. Some ladies came to Sisters Bruner and Cryer while they knelt, and brushed off the water, saying, 'There, there, never mind.' We didn't mind; we shouted and praised the Lord and leaped for joy. Oh, glory to God!

"When we got up, the woman who kept the place came out and took hold of Brother Cryer and me and gave us a shaking apiece, which helped our joy a little more. Glory to God! She then went after the policeman, and we thought we might have a chance to go to jail. We were on what we thought was the street, but which we found was paved land belonging to the public house. The policeman asked us to please move into the street, and we did so, and our meeting went on in the Spirit.

"Oh, how I feel God's power coming on me. I would like to be 'one' for every land. I see the need so in Norway, in England, in Africa, and in America that I would like to be in EVERY LAND. My heart is with the dear workers in America and together we will conquer. God is with us.

"The grandest victory we have had on our journey we shouted over in Liverpool. The first soul to die the death to carnality and receive the Holy Ghost and fire was a sister in Liverpool, Mrs. M——. She has been seeking a long time and has nearly been in despair. Four weeks ago when we preached in Liverpool she was fasting and praying all day and did not come out to meetings. Her hired girl was out, and when the meeting was over she hastened home and told her mistress that two American missionaries were at meeting and from what they preached she (the hired girl) was not saved. Then she broke down and sobbed. Her mistress told her to calm herself and tell her what the men had said. Then she told her that we had said that God would destroy all the self-life and

that it must die; that we said she must confess the carnal
nature to God and that God could destroy the carnal self
in an instant.   The sister said: 'I am very glad. that is
what I want.'

"She went to praying more earnestly than ever and at
midnight the next day she came through shouting victory.
She at once went to testifying and in a number of places
in the city began to tell them what she had found.   How
God has led her out! and how clear is the light of God on
our path!   She received all alone in Liverpool just what I
got in Marengo, Illinois.   The maid has not yet got the
blessing, but is seeking earnestly.

"The leader of a mission work, an Episcopalian clergy-
man, is also seeking the DEATH to the carnal mind.   How
our souls have been lightened over this glorious victory.
Sister M—— has also been healed of a cancer.   Let us all
praise the Lord.   "VIVIAN A. DAKE."

ENROUTE TO AFRICA

"November 14th found Brother Chapman and myself
on board the steamship *Kinsembo*, bound for Monrovia,
Africa.   This is the same boat that Brother and Sister
Chapman went over in, two years ago.   When they were
safely landed, on the return voyage, the boat ran into a
rock near Sierra Leone, and sank in thirteen feet of water.
She was raised and repaired and has been doing good work
ever since.   She is twenty years old, but rides the steadiest
of any ship I have ever sailed on.

"We have had a very pleasant voyage.   Have passed
the Bay of Biscay and are now on the African coast within
a few hours of the Grand Canary Islands.   Bishop Taylor
is among the passengers.   He is very genial and approach-
able.   I have had several good talks with him.   One night
he came into our cabin and we talked a while, then we pro-

posed prayer, and he repeated a chapter and we had a good time on our knees.

"Sabbath, November 15th. The Bishop preached in the first cabin saloon from 'Search the Scriptures.' God is with us. I arise early and go on the forecastle deck and have an hour with God, consequently my soul is watered and refreshed all the day. When I think of the souls saved and sanctified and the watch-fires kindled already on the trip, I am a thousand times glad that God opened my way to come. I want to preach this clean salvation in every land and tongue. I have learned to say 'Lovet vera Gude,' which is the Norwegian for 'Blessed be God!' and if I can get a note of victory in Kru or Mandingo at Monrovia, I shall find it. All Hail! Hallelujah!

"Africa's shores are in sight. Hallelujah! Many times I have sung: 'Afric's shores I long to see,' but now I see them. The low sea coast is in sight. We are this Friday, November 27th, drawing up to Goree in Senegal, one of the French possessions. I shall soon tread African soil, as we are expecting to go ashore in the third officer's boat when he lands the mail. We have had a very pleasant trip down from the Canary Islands. It is just warm enough to be pleasant, like delightful June weather. We are now farther south than any point of the United States, and we still go farther south. We shall not reach Monrovia until December 4th, making twenty days on the trip from Liverpool.

"While ashore on the Grand Canary Islands last Monday, we went to get some milk. We could not find a milk-shop anywhere. So a Spanish boy led us back on the mountain in the edge of the town to a cow farm. The man came up from the field and got two mugs and milked us each some. After ten days of ship fare we relished the milk very much. On this island the poor people live in caves in the hillside. It is always spring here, so that any place that keeps out the rain is quite comfortable.

"But, oh, how they need the gospel. The climate of these islands is wonderful. They raise cochineal, corn, beans, potatoes, peaches, apples, bananas, figs, oranges, lemons, guavas, dates, sweet potatoes, caladium esculentum, and sugar-cane. Cows and sheep abound. I can not tell how much this journey is firing my soul. I feel the spirit of Paul, Judson, Carey, and our blessed Lord, increasing on me. 'Go ye into all the world and preach the gospel to every creature.'

"Four p. m. While the ship lay anchored at Goree, which is an island with French forts on it, a boat load of passengers sailed over to Daka on the mainland two miles away. This is a town of several hundred inhabitants, a French military station. The people belong to the Joliffe tribe. There are no churches here but Catholic and Mohammedan. The caravans from the Sahara desert come down here. They also have a narrow-gauge railway into the interior. How my soul longs for a missionary for Daka.

"I saw the Mohammedans with their Koran, and the Catholic priest with his beads. The climate is quite healthful. They raise many peanuts. I measured a stack 36x25 feet, and about ten feet high. A missionary could do good work here, and soon make a way into the interior. The Joliffe people are quite a bright people. Who hears the Macedonian cry? Men are needed all along this continent whose hearts are on fire, and who are willing to be spent for God. We will be in Bathurst, Senegambia, in the morning, D. V.

"Bathurst is the principal town of the English possession called Senegambia. It is situated a few miles from the mouth of the Gambia river. The river here is about three miles wide. The land is flat and sandy. This is an old trading port. It is more healthful than at Monrovia. Here we saw African huts for the first time. The bamboo huts with their thatched roofs were plentiful. Above them stretched up the long trunks of the cocoanut palm trees loaded with cocoanuts. Orange trees abound.

"On Sabbath day Brother Fennele, the British Wesleyan missionary, came to the ship in the governor's boat, and took Sisters Wilcox and Carlson, Brother Chapman and myself to town to meeting at his chapel. Bishop Taylor had already gone ashore. The chapel is large, holding about six hundred people. The bishop preached from 1 John 1:9.

"After service Brother Chapman and I went out on the street and found a group of Mohammedans, and preached Jesus Christ to them. They asked how God could die, and we then explained to them that Christ died to satisfy a broken law. The blessing of God came on us. Glory to His name! While we were busy with these a young boy came up and asked us to go to his house and read the Bible to him. We went, and he led us to a typical African hut. An orange tree loaded with large oranges bloomed above it. We read and sang and prayed with them. There were four African women in the family.

"We took dinner with Brother Fennele. Bishop Taylor and the two sisters were also present. Sister Sarah Wilcox preached in the evening from John 3:14, 15. The large chapel was well filled. Oh, how they sang at the conclusion. The altar was crowded with seekers for pardon and purity. Some were really convicted. We felt that had they been held to separation from the world a good work could have been done. It avails but little to urge seekers to accept Christ who have not given up the world, whether they be civilized or heathen. Three or four professed to be saved. The governor's boat carried us back to the *Kinsembo,* and we speedily found our way to our stateroom and to rest.

"Bathurst has had Methodist preaching for fifty years. The people love the truth but are very worldly. The same laxity in enforcing Discipline is as apparent here as in our own land. Jewelry, feathers, flowers, and gaudy dressing abound. But a grand work could be done here by one who would let the Holy Ghost have His way.

"This is the most fruitful field for immediate work I have seen. There are now Catholics, members of the Church of England, Mohammedans, and British Wesleyans here. From Bathurst to Freetown, the capital of Sierra Leone, is two days' journey. The weather became much warmer as we approached Sierra Leone.

"One day the Mohammedans on board had an interesting religious ceremony. The priest wrote some verses from the Koran on a piece of paper. Then he washed the words off the paper in some water. Then he took condensed milk and mixed with the water and passed it around, and all drank the milk of the Koran. How unsatisfactory this inky milk to ease the troubled soul! But, thank God, the follower of Jesus can get the milk of the Word. Can not we learn from these poor idolaters a lesson of reverence for the Word of God? and may we not be inspired to more continuously drink it?

"We saw sharks to day, those plunderers of the deep. How like are they to the devil, always on the lookout for prey. No poor man who comes within their reach but feels the sharp teeth of these fierce scavengers. The only safety is to keep out of Satan's reach.

"To-day I had a talk with the bishop on missionary work and its hindrances. The greatest, he said, was the unhealthful climate which caused the death of many of his missionaries. The bishop is over seventy years old, but hale and strong yet. Like Moses 'his eye is not dim nor his natural force abated.' He is one of the most childlike men I ever met in my life. He is quite patriarchial in appearance and is without doubt one of the most radical, thorough, aggressive teachers in the Methodist Episcopal church. God has evidently fitted him for the work he is doing, which is doubtless the most Scriptural in the church. His consecration is great. He leaves his wife and family in America and spends most of his life in Africa.

"Sierre Leone is a British possession north of Liberia, and its capital is Freetown. It lies at the foot of a group of mountains. The highest one is fifteen hundred feet. We went ashore here and were very hospitably entertained by Brother Jaderquist, and other of the first Soudan missionaries. God sweetly blest us here, and we shouted the praises of God. We saw many things that we had not seen before. We ate mango plums and pawpaws, which we found quite good.

"We were soon on our journey and in due time Cape Mesurado came in view, and soon we could see Monrovia at the foot and on the side of the hill.

AT THE CAPITAL OF LIBERIA

"We landed about five p. m., November 18th. You can all imagine our meeting with Sister Chapman, after she had been here alone for seven months. She was quite well, although she had had the fever lately. The mission house is surrounded by 'bush' and tropical trees. Among those I can see from the window are banana, orange, lime, mango plum, cocoanut, breadnut, pawpaw, butter pear, coffee and plantain trees.

"There are at present four children in the home, two Congo girls, Susie and Maggie, Frank, a Bassa boy, Lewis, a Vey. Then there are three boys at work, Thomas, a Pessa, Sirsy, a Pusa, and Joe, a Gola. After prayers I took Thomas out in the 'bush' and talked and prayed with him. God broke my heart all down as I held him up to a throne of grace. Then he prayed God to forgive him. He said: 'O God, take my old, bad heart, give me new heart.' Will all pray God to answer this prayer? He is a bright boy and could be very useful. We are praying God to save him. We will not limit God. We believe He can save here as well as anywhere. Amen. We are holding on to God to send us a revival.

"Have been much blessed in secret prayer since arriving in Africa, and have a good, strong hold on God for victory in the various fields. Two weeks of African life have given me more insight into the needs of the field than months of correspondence. Sister Chapman has some native children here whom she is earnestly endeavoring to train for God.

"I have been to the cemetery and have seen the graves of our dear missionaries, Mattie North, Jennie Torrence, and Sumner Kerwood. They lie near each other. I felt no sorrow for their death as I stood there. I am glad their warfare is ended, and they are safe in heaven. Their work here has not been in vain. Doubters and fault-finders will yet see that God has received glory from their lives and deaths.

"December 11th. I went in a log canoe up the St. Paul river to the Lutheran mission kept by Brother and Sister Day. Had a very pleasant ride. It was novel to glide along the river in a canoe impelled by the vigorous strokes of our Bassa boys. The scenery on the St. Paul river is very fine. The mission station is on a commanding hill-top. It is surrounded by thousands of coffee trees, and many other tropical species. The river rapids make music day and night. We were received in the most hospitable manner possible. While we could see the need of a deeper piety, more secret prayer and a more sober walking with God, yet we never saw hospitality that equalled theirs. We found them literally 'given to hospitality.'

"I have been in many a house where I felt I was one too many, but here everything in the house was at the visitor's pleasure. Sick and well are equally welcome. All the sick missionaries at the coast come here and are tenderly nursed without money or price. God bless great-hearted Brother and Sister Day and Brother Goll. An American scientific expedition was quartered here when we arrived and the house was full, but we were as warmly received as though we were the only guests, and no hint was given that they were crowded. God helped in preaching His Word on Sabbath to a mixed gathering of scientists, missionaries, mission children, and native Golahs and Pessas, the latter of whom did not understand even the simplest words. My own soul was well watered.

"On Tuesday, Brother and Sister Day fitted us out with ten boys and provisions for a twelve-mile walk back among the natives. We started early, crossed the river in a canoe, and were soon single file on the path. We passed native villages deserted in the war that had just closed between the Golahs and Mandingos. We arrived at Henry's town, our destination, about eleven a. m.

"This town is located on the bank of a beautiful, cold stream that flows all the year round. Mount Coffee is close at hand. We went up on the mountain and saw some yellow and gray monkeys in the trees. Parrots and deer are also seen here. We slept in a native house on a bamboo bed, and ate from a bamboo mat. Each night we had service. It was a strange scene. The fire burning in the center of the town, the natives, almost naked, eagerly listening to 'God-palaver' (as they call preaching), the mud huts with their roofs of leaves, etc. Henry Stewart, the head man of the town, is one of Brother Day's mission boys.

"We stayed two days and then made our way back to Brother Day's homelike mission. On the 18th we took the little steamer that runs down the river and returned to our home in Monrovia. Found Brother and Sister Chapman usually well. We expect to commence meetings in the Methodist Episcopal church the evening of December 20th. The needs of this work are great. We want to do more than we are able without the help of God's people."

"December 12th. About forty raw heathen had a "pala-ver' to-day at the mission house and Brother Day gave them each a yard of overall stuff for some work they had done. They were of the Pessa tribe, nearly naked, and had their hair shaved back to about the middle of their heads. I have been real blest to-day."

"December 13th. Preached twice to-day in the mission chapel, and was blessed. Especially in the evening I had a real touch from God. My soul was melted at the thought of the wondrous love of Jesus. I felt extra well after preaching twice and sweating profusely in this hot climate. My audience was all sizes and conditions, from the edu-cated white man to the raw heathen."

"December 18th. To-day after good-bys we took the little steamboat, the *Sarah Ann,* for Cape Mesurado. We had a pleasant ride. Six miles this side of Monrovia our steamer struck on a sand bar and we rode into town in a surf boat."

"December 20th. This evening I commenced meetings in the Methodist Episcopal church of Monrovia. There was a good turnout and a shaking among the people. The Lord helped me much in preaching from Jeremiah 21:5."

"December 21st. A steamer from home came in last night and we got our mail this morning. We got the news of the death of Grace Hill, our teacher in the Reaper's Home. She was a choice spirit, sober-minded and always bent on doing God's will. She has gone to her reward. I found a steamer would return January 23rd, when I ex-pect to sail for England. We had a good meeting at six a. m., in our bamboo church at Krootown. I was much helped in preaching at night in the Methodist Episcopal church. We hold two services every day, one at Krootown in the morning, and in the Methodist Episcopal church at night. A lady came forward without invitation to-night. My soul was watered, though God gave truth which did not bring many 'amens.' "

"December 22nd. At Krootown we had a good crowd. They were very attentive to the truth and I believe some are under conviction. A good time in the meeting at night."

"December 23rd. I talked to the Kroo men from the parable of the sower. Neka and Nimla, two head members, were at the altar, and then came to the Band home and we had prayers together. Preached with liberty at night."

"December 24th. Brother Chapman and I got a canoe to-day and went to Barnersville. We went up Stackton Creek four and a half miles, and then turned off into another creek and went to its source. It was a fine ride. We found a nice country. We had prayers with Mr. Howard Tyler, an American negro, who came over thirteen years ago, and was the first settler at Barnersville. We passed thirty-six canoes in coming back."

"December 25th. This is the strangest Christmas I ever spent. I am in a tropical land. The birds are singing in the evergreen trees and the trees are loaded with fruit. Plums, pears, cocoanuts, bananas, plantain, pawpaws, cherries, oranges, limes, and lemons await the picker. The weather is very hot. I prayed and received my Christmas gift, a most blessed baptism of the Holy Ghost. I prayed for all the workers by name, and got so blessed I leaped for joy and ran through the house. Had a good time at Krootown this morning and in the Methodist Episcopal church at night."

"December 26th. Went to Krootown and felt God's blessing on me. I talked to them from the parable of the barren fig tree. No meeting at the Methodist Episcopal church to-night."

"December 27th. I went to the Holiness Band meeting at six a. m., led the meeting and had a blessed time in holding up the light. I went to the Presbyterian church at eleven a. m. and gave them a talk; to Krootown in the afternoon and had a good turnout and God's presence. At

night I had a blessed time using the parable of the rich
man and Lazarus. Have been struggling with fever all
day and to-night was feeling bad. Brother Chapman gave
me a cold water pack. The Lord blest me and I got quite
easy. This is my first experience with African fever."

"December 28th. I feel some better this forenoon
though my head still aches. I got melted to tears over
Isaac Watts' hymn:

> 'Lord, how secure and blest are they
> Who feel the joys of pardoned sin.'

The sweetness of heaven came into my soul. Oh, how safe
I feel. Bless the Lord! A text on the wall is about me
like a defense, 'The Lord is my light and my salvation,
whom shall I fear.' A gracious watering of God's Holy
Spirit helped me soul and body."

STRICKEN WITH AFRICAN FEVER

For some time before leaving America it had been evident to Mr. Dake's nearest friends that his superhuman
efforts were carrying him fast to the river's brink. He
seemed to feel it himself, and often spoke of going. He
said to the workers: "If any of you are near when I die,
have me buried on the field where I fall, and shout over
my triumph, rather than weep over my departure, as you
rush on after the lost."

He was taken with the dread African fever on Monday,
December 28th, 1891, at the mission house of Brother and
Sister Chapman, Monrovia, Africa. From a letter written
by Sister Chapman after his death, we quote the following: "He was taken down one week ago to-day, was better the next day, but we felt he was taking the African
fever, and as he was very much run down, we advised him
to get ready to start for England on a steamer then a week
overdue. The fever ran pretty high Saturday, but all

thought it would be best for him to go, and get the sea air and into a cooler atmosphere as soon as possible."

He was carried on board the steamer by native men, and left under the care of Mr. Smirl, a missionary from the Methodist Episcopal seminary, and Mr. Brownell, a scientific explorer, both of whom were taking the steamer for England. Henry, a converted native, accompanied Mr. Dake, who intended he should be educated and trained for missionary work in Africa. Brother Buckwalter, of Bishop Taylor's mission, and Brother Chapman, who had been very attentive to Mr. Dake, and nursed him through his sickness thus far, went on board and made all necessary preparations for his journey. We can not do better than to insert Mr. Brownell's letter in full, written on shipboard.

HIS DEATH AND BURIAL

"Ship *Mandingo,* January 10, 1892.
"Mrs. V. A. Dake,

Dear Madam: Having been with your husband much of late, I feel it my duty to write you as fully as I can concerning him. I know not whether you have heard the sad news as yet; if not I will say at first that he died at Sierre Leone, January 5, 1892, of African fever. He had been sick nine days, and died while delirious. He was taken sick on Monday, December 28th, at Mr. Chapman's, in Monrovia. They kept him there till next steamer, which was on the following Saturday. Mr. Smirl and I also took that boat. We boarded the ship about midnight, as they were to sail before daylight and did not arrive before evening. Mr. Dake was carried in an invalid chair by natives. We had then to take surfboat about a quarter of a mile to the ship. He remained in the chair and was carefully hoisted into the ship, and placed in a berth in the same room as

Mr. Smirl and myself. He felt well and very cheerful.
Next morning, Sunday, he felt very well indeed, and was
jubilant in the thought of soon reaching a temperate clime.
The ship's physician, who had not been to see him the night
before, said: 'Why, you are all right. I expected to see
a sick man.' He did indeed appear to be done with the
fever.

"He said that his back was healthy as a baby's, and his
stomach the same. His temperature was almost normal.
Next morning he was worse and had considerable fever.
He had taken no medicine at Mr. Chapman's, except wet
packs. The doctor on the ship insisted that he take medicine or he would be put ashore at Sierre Leone, as he was
responsible for his life. Accordingly he took several doses
of quinine, and one or two other medicines.

"We reached Sierre Leone about noon on Monday, and
Mr. Smirl and I went ashore for oranges and limes, leaving him in charge of Henry, the black boy whom he had
decided to take with him to America. We returned in a
few hours, having called on the missionary residing there,
named McCullough. We found Mr. Dake feeling about
the same. Toward evening Mr. McCullough came off in a
boat to see Mr. Dake. It seems he and Mr. Chapman had
stopped at his home on their way out to Liberia. He had
not been able to sleep for several nights, and was given a
sleeping draught at 10 o'clock Monday evening. Monday
night he slept but little. At five o'clock in the morning, I
was awakened by Mr. Smirl calling me loudly. I jumped
from my berth to see Mr. Smirl and Henry holding Mr.
Dake, who was calling loudly, and trying to get out of bed.
We soon got him back, but he remained delirious until one
o'clock p. m., when he passed quietly away. I was in the
room when he passed away, and so quiet was it that I
could not tell the exact moment of his death.

"We immediately sent word to Mr. McCullough to see
if he could arrange to have him buried on shore, as our

ship left in a few hours and he would have to be buried that night at sea. Soon Mr. McCullough came and had a coffin brought. He was wrapped in a sheet placed carefully in the coffin, and carried ashore. Our ship then left. You will hear the rest from Mr. McCullough. He was resigned all the time and felt that God was teaching him some great lesson. His things were immediately sealed up, and the captain is responsible for them. To say that I sympathize with you in this great sorrow would be a very slight expression of my feeling. But I believe as you do in an overruling Providence and I believe he is much better off than ever before. May God bless you, my dear sister, is my earnest prayer.

"Very truly yours,
"GEO. G. BROWNELL."

"Freetown, West Coast, Africa, January 18, 1892.
"DEAR BROTHER CHAPMAN:

"I hardly know just what to say; but presume you have been made aware of the calling home of our Brother Dake on board the steamer *Mandingo,* on the 5th instant. Brother Dake passed sweetly away with a smile on his face. When the steamer arrived here it was reported to leave in a few hours and it was shortly before the time set for leaving that I was informed of Brother Dake's presence and illness on the steamer. I went on board and did what I could, but had to leave soon because the steamer expected to go, it being about seven o'clock p. m. The next morning I was surprised to learn the steamer was still in harbor. I had a fever patient in our house, Brother Codding, to look after, and as the steamer was expected to go at any time, I did not go on board in the morning. About three p. m. word was sent me that Brother Dake had passed away about one o'clock p. m. I immediately took charge of affairs and brought the body ashore and

had the funeral the next morning at eight o'clock. The
captain of the steamer took charge of the personal effects
of Brother Dake and said he would turn them over to the
proper authorities in Liverpool. He gave me £4 to cover
expenses here, and of this sum nine shillings are left. The
grave of our departed Brother will need some stones put
around it to keep it from sinking down when the wet
weather comes. This will cost four or five shillings. The
rules of the country are as follows: For a temporary mark
over a grave, a mark for one year, ten shillings. For a
permanent mark, thirty shillings. This is just a license to
mark the grave; the material for the work and the labor
of making it is extra. Brother Dake left no message behind. When I saw him the day the steamer arrived I did
not think he was dangerously ill. I thought if the vessel ran out into cooler air that he would get along all
right. I was told that he became delirious that night and
had scarcely any rational moments afterwards. He talked
of his wife and children a good deal. Sometime before
the end he fell into a comatose state, which continued
until the last.   "ALLEN McCULLOUGH."

MEMORIAL SERVICES

Mr. Dake's many friends manifested their sympathy
for his bereaved family by the tender letters of condolence
to us and through the religious journals of the country.
A memorial service in commemoration of his death was
held in Muhlenburg Mission, January 17, 1892, by Rev.
A. E. Day, of the Lutheran church. Another service of this
kind was held in the Mission of Love, Liverpool, England,
February 11th, 1892, by Rev. Herbert Wood, of the Church
of England. A third was held at Kempton, Illinois, April
17th, by the Peoria district of the Illinois conference, Rev.
F. D. Brooke presiding. A fourth one was held by the

members of Chicago First Church, May 26th, O. V. Ketels, pastor. The fifth was held by the Pentecost Bands at their annual Harvest Home camp-meeting at Newton, Iowa, July 31st, at which Thos. H. Nelson presided. Next, the Illinois conference, convened at Elgin, Illinois, and of which Mr. Dake was a member, held a memorial service October 9th, presided over by President B. T. Roberts, who so soon followed him to rest and reward. These memorial services were times of great blessing, especially the last one. Many interesting incidents relative to Mr. Dake's fervent piety and faithful labors were related as tributes to his memory. All seemed to feel that a "prince in Israel" had fallen, especially his workers and the brethren of his conference.

Rev. S. K. Wheatlake wrote on his death the following lines:

> He fainted on the battlefield,
> Secure behind faith's trusty shield;
> With armor on the warrior fell,
> Unsmitten by the darts of hell.
>
> He fell beneath meridian sun,
> At noon a full day's work was done.
> No more he treads the battleground,
> No more the cross—he wears the crown.
>
> No more he'll join us in the fight
> Against the wrong for God and right.
> Close up the breach in which he stood,
> Be bold to strike or die for God.
>
> Oft we were blest, 'mid battle roar,
> To hear him shout his victories o'er,
> And when his sword flashed forth the light,
> We waxed more valiant in the fight.
>
> Gird up your loins. No longer weep.
> God giveth His beloved sleep.
> Soon far beyond the battle fray,
> We'll meet on coronation day.

But hark! hear ye that battle cry,
Stand firm, the hellish foe is nigh;
With Spirit's sword and victor's song,
Quit you like men. In God be strong.

FROM G. W. CHAPMAN

"Monrovia, Africa, December 21, 1892.

"In reply to your request I send you some reminiscen-
ces of the last days of Rev. V. A. Dake: On November
14th, 1891, he and I left England for Africa. He spent
most of his time reading his Bible and the lives of Dr.
Adam Clarke, Bishop Coke, and others. He spoke of
Bishop Coke dying on his way to India as a missionary
and intimated that the Lord would take him on this trip,
but as I did not believe it he attributed it to a temptation
from the enemy. Yet he seemed to retain an inner conviction that he would never see his wife again, of whom he
spoke in the most affectionate terms.

"He asked me what I would do if he should die. I
told him I would go on the same with our work. He said:
'That is what I want you to do.' He expressed himself
thus, that if God took him, he wanted the Pentecost Band
work to go on the same. He would not say much about
his dying for fear it would discourage me.

"Every morning at daybreak or before he would go to
the bow of the boat and pray. He would break down and
cry to God in agony of soul as though a lost world was on
his heart. We reached Monrovia, December 5th, 1891.
The next day we attended the Methodist Episcopal class
meeting. Here Brother Dake testified to God's saving
power with his heart melted before the Lord. His testimony was like an oasis in the desert to those who knew the
joyful sound. We had some native men working for us
and he began to labor with them immediately. He would

pray and weep over them as though they were his own children.

"He went to Mr. Day's mission twenty-five miles from Monrovia and stayed a few days, returning December 18th. He commenced a meeting in the Methodist Episcopal church and preached every night for a week, holding one during the same time in the morning at Krootown. There was quite an interest manifested among the heathen and some professed to be saved. Brother Dake prayed for them with a burdened and longing heart to see them raised out of heathen darkness.

"I never saw a preacher or missionary who had such great love for souls. On Sunday night, December 27th, 1891, he preached the last sermon that he ever delivered, in the Methodist Episcopal church in Monrovia, from Luke 16:19. He dwelt mostly on the latter clause of the text, 'He fared sumptuously every day.' He warned his hearers of living in luxury and for this world. He ended his discourse with a heartfelt appeal to them to arouse from their lethargy. He had a little fever while preaching and continued to get worse.

"On January 2, 1892, we took him on the English homeward bound steamer at ten o'clock at night and laid him in his berth. We thought it best for him to go and get the sea air. He took me by the hand and said: 'God be with you till we meet again;' then said: 'George, meet me in glory.' And we parted to meet no more on earth. During his sickness he would frequently get out of bed, fall on his knees and pray. He lived each hour ready for his Master's coming."

FROM REV. G. H. AGNEW, MISSIONARY

"Inhambane, E. Africa, June 10, 1892.

"Like others I was, of course, greatly surprised to hear of the departure for glory of our beloved Brother Dake.

It seems strange that one so eminently useful, such a burning and shining light, should be taken and we be left behind. He was the first, and I believe the best, Free Methodist preacher I knew. When he first came into the store where I was in St. Paul, Minnesota, he took me by the hand and inquired about my soul's welfare. I felt attached to him at once. He was at this time chairman of the Minnesota and Northern Iowa conference. It is now eight years since he took me into the church. I have never regretted that step. I can never regret having come into church fellowship with such people as he represented.

"At the time Brother Dake visited me at St. Paul, there was another brother associated with me in business, who was also a professed Christian. In conversation with Brother Dake at one time a thought struck him and he exclaimed, 'Oh, wait until I tell you a joke,' or words to that effect, but without waiting for what was coming, Brother Dake said, 'I never joke. Let us pray,' and dropped immediately upon his knees.

"Many preachers would have listened to the joke, laughed and added another one to it, but this was not his style. He had no time for jesting, but was a man of God, reproving, rebuking, exhorting with all long-suffering, all intent on getting souls to the blood and believers to the fountain of cleansing.

"Any one traveling with him on railroad cars, etc., could not fail to see how interested he was in the salvation of others, giving out tracts, quoting Scripture, sometimes standing up before a whole carload of passengers and repeating: 'It is appointed unto men once to die, but after this the judgment,' exhorting men and women to become reconciled to God.

"I shall never forget the first and only Harvest Home camp-meeting I attended. I went there a carnally-minded man, although like many others imagining I was all right. Brother Dake's exhortations to get clean scorched like fire, but the 'old man' inside would hide, although there was a restlessness within which, at times, was painful. However, God let me see myself in all my natural loathfulness, and I began in earnest to cry for deliverance from the body of death. A few minutes before I got through Brother Dake came into the tent where I was and caught me by the shoulders, giving me a gentle shaking. This was the point. I saw, as it were, God waiting to deliver me; I was waiting to be delivered and Brother Dake was anxious I should get through. A cry that reached the throne came from me and the work of entire cleansing was done. Brother Dake seemed about as blest over it for the time as I was myself. This was the beginning of almost a new life to me. I was then in perfect harmony with all those who were cleansed, which I never had been before.

"I loved to be in the company of all those who had reached the rock, and especially was I glad whenever I had an opportunity of being with our beloved brother, who always gave me, as it were, new strength for the battle against sin."

"Muhlenburg Mission, West Coast, Africa,
September 1st, 1892.

"MY DEAR SISTER:

"It is not on account of any lack of interest or sympathy for you in your great bereavement that I have been so tardy in writing to you. Ever since we heard of the death of your dear husband I have had it in my mind to write. I had read his writings and sung his hymns so much that I felt I knew him. His name, through the *Vanguard* and Brother and Sister Chapman, became familiar to us long before he came to Africa and we saw him face to face and had the rare pleasure of having him with us in our own home.

"As I now recall the event and the precious memories

of the songs he sang, the edifying conversation and his earnest, soul-thrilling, uplifting prayers, all seem to have special messages from God. I can not now hear some of the hymns he sang and taught us while here without feeling my heart growing larger and my desire for souls more earnest.

"Yes, Brother Dake's short stay among us was fraught with help and blessing to all. While he was here, one day when I went into the room where he was sitting at the table writing, that serene, heavenly, restful calm seemed to have settled down over his face, giving him the expression of one from some other sphere, where cares, sickness, pain and weariness of flesh are unknown. He was sitting there writing and, looking up with a smile, said to me: 'Sister Day, I have written some verses; here they are. Shall I read them to you?' Of course I said yes. After he got through and I expressed my pleasure in them he said: 'They are for you if you care for them.' 'Yes, indeed,' I said; 'nothing would please me more.' He said he wanted to do something for me. I was always so busy and doing something for him. I considered it the greatest pleasure to minister to him and all of God's workers whom we have the pleasure of entertaining.

"I will send you the verses in his own hand to see if you wish to copy them or have them printed. You can do so and then, if it will not be too much to ask you, kindly return them, as I prize them the more because they were written, not printed. Praying God's blessing and care for you and your dear little ones, and the work which lay so near Brother Dake's heart, I am your friend and sister in the Master's service,   "Sincerely,

"MRS. E. L. DAY.

On the following page are the verses referred to in Mrs. Day's letter:

"MUHLENBURG MISSION STATION"

"Beautiful for situation,
Muhlenburg, the mission station,
On the highlands by the river,
Where the sungod from his quiver
Shoots his arrows bright and shining,
All the life-germs quick divining,
And by death the life quick bringing
With his arrows sharp and stinging.
Loudly roars the rapid river,
Praises singing to the Giver
Of its purity and motion,
Leading us to true devotion.
Round about the habitation
Springs the tropic vegetation;
Palm trees with their crowns of glory,
Subjects they of song and story,
And bananas golden cluster,
And the pawpaw yellow luster,
Lime trees with the fruit refreshing
And the oranges possessing
Satisfaction for the weary.
Coffee trees with ruddy berries,
 Mango plums and pears and cherries;
These and many other furnish
Cheer, life's joy to brightly burnish.

Planted here from sternest duty,
'Mid these scenes of passing beauty,
'Neath the glorious light of heaven,
And the thousand blessings given,
But here death's darts fly unceasing,
Dangers evermore increasing;
And as martyrs in the fire,
Heard their Master say, 'Come higher,'
Counted not their lives their treasure,
Winning Christ's eternal pleasure,
Go these Christians who here labor
For their long-lost heathen neighbor,
Risk their lives their souls to lighten,
Give their all their night to brighten,
Cut their lives off prematurely,

That the light of heaven securely
Here may blaze like beacon station
On a dark and heathen nation.
Like the ships on stormy ocean,
Sinking midst the wild commotion,
Sights afar the lighthouse burning,
Toward the haven joyful turning,
So light from this mission streaming,
On the darkened heathen beaming,
Gathers them from every station;
And they come to hear of Jesus,
Who alone from sin can free us.
Only mightier prayer prevailing,
And a faith that knows no failing,
Will bring more from sin's dominion,
Changed in heart as in opinion.
But when sick, with life in danger,
This the harbor for the stranger.
Here he finds a sister, brother,
Love of father and of mother
Poured out on him without measure,
From their hearts' unstinting treasure.
While to all is due this mention
There is one to whom attention
Should be called in faithful numbers,
One who neither sleeps nor slumbers
But pours out her life like water;
Like the Master, is His daughter
In her care for every stranger
In the lovely land of danger.
God hath taken all her treasures
To a land of heavenly pleasures,
And her heart by this hath broken,
As His Word hath truly spoken,
Whom the Lord doth love He chastens,
And His own work thus He hastens;
Cuts the earthly love asunder,
Leaves the soul in weeping wonder.
As the rose when bruised is sweetest,
And the gold and silver meetest,
When its dross removed by fire,
Fits it for a purpose higher,
So the soul refined by trial,

Scorched by wrath's severest vial,
Shines as ministering angel
On continuous evangel.
And the thoughtful note the dealing
Of our God His love revealing,
And anew the story tell,
Jesus doeth all things well.
May the blessing of our God
Soften thus the chastening rod
To our friends, we humbly pray,
Till all night is lost in day."

CHAPTER VI

LETTERS OF CONDOLENCE

North Chili, February 11, 1892.

MY DEAR SISTER DAKE:

I feel very sad over the sorrowful tidings just received. It does not seem possible that our dear Brother Dake has left us so suddenly for his mansion in the skies. Like Summerfield, who died at the age of twenty-seven, he was consumed by a burning yearning for the salvation of souls. We mourn his loss. We sympathize with you in this deep affliction. Few women have lost such a husband; few churches have lost such a preacher. I appreciate his greatness and his goodness and I feel that his life of self-sacrifice, of disinterested devotion and of consuming zeal has been an encouragement and an inspiration to me to press on with greater diligence in the narrow way. He has led the way to brighter worlds, and beckons us onward and upward.

May the Everlasting Arms be round about you and your fatherless children, and may you be sustained and comforted with special manifestations of Infinite Love.

You must look upon me as a father and a friend and be free to call upon me for any service that I can render you or yours. Mrs. Roberts joins in love and sympathy.

Yours in Jesus' love,

B. T. ROBERTS.

[This article was written by Brother Roberts for the *Free Methodist*].

VIVIAN A. DAKE

With a multitude of God's children we feel deeply afflicted over the death of our dear brother and son in the Gospel.

He came to our school at Chili, a bright, uncultivated, unconverted boy, thirsting for knowledge, ambitious to learn.

He was clearly converted and at once became a power for good. His religion was not of the quiet, unemphatic kind. The love of

Christ was like a fire shut up in his bones. With others he went from house to house wherever it was acceptable, and sang, and prayed, and exhorted, and endeavored to win souls to Christ, and to help them on in the kingdom of grace. After graduating at Chili Seminary he entered the Rochester University. He maintained a creditable standing in his studies, and not only kept his religious fervor, but his ardor for soul-saving became so intense that he felt he could not stay to finish his collegiate course; so he left and entered the ministry.

When on a circuit he did not feel satisfied with simply filling his appointments, but kept revival fires burning all around him. As a chairman he did the work of an evangelist and kept the current of salvation flowing all the while. As the organizer and director of the Pentecost Bands his work is well known. It would be difficult to find a class of young men and women more fully consecrated to God, more self-denying, more filled with holy zeal, more thorough in their work, more ready to lay down their lives for Christ than these Pentecost workers. They have fully demonstrated that to reach the masses no instrumental music, no carnal methods are necessary.

Brother Dake was a man of uncommon ability, of rare devotion to Christ and His work, and of untiring zeal. He was a prodigious worker, and his superhuman efforts have proved too great for his mortal body. He will be mourned by thousands, and the world will be a loser by his death.

He who could rally around him such soldiers of the cross, and keep them on the battlefield, was no ordinary man. We trust that his example of zeal for winning souls will be an inspiration and an encouragement to all our preachers to devote themselves wholly to God and His work.

Under the chastening influence of this great affliction all hearts given to God should be drawn together, all past differences should be forgotten, and with one heart and one mind we should exert all our energies to win souls to Christ.   B. T. R.

P. S.—The sad news of the death of Brother Dake reached our office on the 11th. The following particulars were given us by Mr. C. E. Smirl, one of Bishop Taylor's missionaries, who was coming to America, and in whose care Brother Dake was placed when leaving Monrovia.

They went on board the steamer at 12 o'clock Saturday night, January 2. The next day Brother Dake was better. It was Brother Smirl's opinion that if the ship had remained at sea he might have lived. But after they entered the harbor at Sierre

Leone the heat was intense and Brother Dake was taken worse.
On Tuesday morning his temperature rose to 110 degrees and he
became very delirious, remaining so until he became unconscious.
Death ended his sufferings at about 1 p. m. It was at first supposed that he must be buried at sea, but word being sent to him,
Rev. Mr. McCullough, of Kansas Mission, came on board and
took his body ashore and buried it.

Before taking the steamer Brother Dake was delirious a part
of the time, and this continued at intervals until early Tuesday
morning, when he grew rapidly worse. A sweet smile rested on
his emaciated features after death had done its work.

Brother Dake expected to recover. When lucid he talked of
future labors for the Master, and spoke often of Sister Dake as
"dear Ida."

Brother Dake was widely known throughout the church, and
his sudden death will be mourned by many true hearts. His sor-
rowing family needs the prayers of God's people. May the infinite Comforter be their strong support, and may his aged parents
who are nearing the end of the race be sustained by the God of
all grace.   B. T. R.

                                    New York, February 9, 1891.
Mrs. Dake:

Dear Madam: The sad news you will get in this and one
written by Mr. George Brownell, from Canary Island, will be a
great strain on you, for I am sure it will be entirely unexpected.
It grieves me very much to have to tell you that your dear husband passed over to the Master on January 5th at one o'clock p. m.
I will not go into details now, for I expect to see you in person in
a few days, and Brother Brownell has no doubt given you all the
details. I will only say that all his effects were handed over to
the captain of the steamer, who put them into the hands of the
United States Consul at Liverpool. This is according to marine
law, and, by writing to him, at your request he will turn them
over to the agents of your Mission, Bywater Tanqueray & Co.,
who, by the kindness of Mr. Mills have promised to so do. Mr.
Mills asked me to give you his most sincere sympathy. He is a
very kind man and will do all he can for you. He is the agent
of the above firm.

Brother Dake was a man with whom by associating I learned
to love. We were together quite a good deal while he was in
Liberia. I did not intend starting home so soon, but he got very

bad with the fever and it was decided for him to take the first steamer, and as there was no one to go with him, I decided to go and do what I could to take care of him. About this time Mr. Brownell came down from the country where he had been down with the fever and took the same steamer, so there were two of us instead of one, and in fact three of us, for Brother Dake decided to take Henry, a native boy, with him. He got off at Sierra Leone. He will, no doubt, speak of his boy Henry in some of his notes which you will find among his things. He had quite a number of curios from Africa, which you will also find when the things arrive.

If there is anything else you would like to know I will tell you when I see you, which will perhaps be the last of this week, as I want to stop several days in Chicago. It is needless for me to say that I sympathize with you, but I do very sincerely.

Brother Dake came to Africa at the Master's command. He came preaching the truth as it is in Christ Jesus, never faltering, but always going forward with a rejoicing heart. He has done what he could and the Master has said, "It is enough, come up higher;" and after all it will only be a short time at most when we shall all follow on. May God give you grace sufficient for this trial of yours, always remembering that God shall wipe away all tears from our eyes and there shall be no more death, neither sorrow nor crying, neither shall there be any more pain, for the former things are passed away.

I remain your Brother in sympathy,

C. E. SMIRL.

Belvidere, Illinois, February 23, 1892.

DEAR SISTER DAKE:

If tears or words could tell you how deeply I sympathize with you, how gladly I would tell you, but, oh! your sorrow is deeper than either tears or language can tell. Precious Sister, God bottles up our tears and pours them out in blessing upon the sinners of the earth. Hundreds to-day are joining in the funeral anthems for the loved, while angels are wondering at the holy triumph that shines out from his redeemed face. Methinks I can see him this hour in raiment of white, with his glorified nature radiant as the stars, singing and shouting with Dr. Redfield and all the blessed saints who have gone before. "All hail the power of Jesus' name." Oh! hallowed bliss—purest delight. Dearest Ida, doesn't your soul catch a glimpse of the holy scene? Yes,

I know it does, but the bereaved heart will ache, and the tears will fall. Oh, Jesus, help!

How rich you are, Sister Ida. Besides Jesus, the precious Christ in heaven, you have got Vivian. No more conference censures, no more perils among false brethren, no more longing for Jesus; his great loving heart can see Him whom he loved so well. No more praying through the "Vail"—what supreme, holy delight! No more evil whispering to tear his great heart into shreds, no more burdens for the lost to break his heart in his agonizing appeals to heaven for mercy for them, no more weariness in fasting and privation to age his form and wrinkle his brow, but forever among the blest—forever, Ida, forever! Praise our God. Do you think he will ever forget the prayers and fastings for Jesus' sake? He can not. Neither will he forget you. Take up the work bravely, carry it nobly; by and by Jesus may send him to escort you home to the Marriage Supper of the Lamb. Hallelujah! Dear Ida, your loss is not wholly your own, all feel that a friend has gone. Tears fall in streams from my eyes when I think there is one gone who used to pray for my unsaved children. How much they've lost. Let us pray for God to let his mantle fall upon some one.

I praise God I can meet him at the judgment, conscious that I have never felt one unkind thought against him nor ever spoken one unkind word. I pray God to bless you and shut you into His arms safe from the adversary.

"Yet in all this Job did not charge God foolishly."

Ever yours, absent or present, in Jesus Christ,

LOTTIE B. CRONK.

CHAPTER VII

TRIBUTES

FROM REV. H. W. FISH

"At the Clyde district camp-meeting held at Weedsport, New York, August 21-27, 1889, Brother Dake was present. He came by invitation of the writer and arrived on the camp-ground on Thursday. The meeting was going on with some interest. That evening he was invited to preach.

"Before he began his sermon he sang (assisted by Rev. F. D. Christie) the hymn beginning with, 'We have gathered to hear of the Savior,' with the chorus, 'Parting to meet again at the judgment.' Awful solemnity came upon the congregation and there could be seen weeping in every direction. He gave out his text from 1 Samuel 28:15, 'God is departed from me.' From the beginning of the sermon until the close sinners were made to feel their wretched condition as none but a man filled with the Spirit of God could make them feel. His appeals to those who were crucifying Christ afresh were very touching. His description of a backslider at the judgment and finally lost in hell will never be forgotten by those present.

"When the invitation was given for seekers the altar was crowded. There was rejoicing on earth and in heaven that night over the prodigals returning home. Many were heard to say: 'That was the most vivid, searching preaching we ever heard.' Again while pastor at Saratoga Springs, New York, in the year 1890, Brother Dake was with us Sunday, October 13th, also Monday and Tuesday evenings. His sermon Sunday morning from Hebrews

12:1, will long be remembered by those present. Many were made to feel that there were weights and besetments about them that hindered their running the race from earth to heaven. Fathers and mothers, old and young, were seen weeping all through the congregation.

"At the close of the sermon the pastor announced that there would be a class meeting after the congregation was dismissed and all that desired could remain. The whole congregation remained. That was a searching time, and under the light of the truth many entered into a more complete consecration to God and the entire abandonment of all those things that savor of the world or indicate the presence of pride.

"The Monday evening meeting was a time of marked victory. After singing and a season of prayer, Brother Dake opened the Bible to his text. He then requested the congregation to join in singing the hymn beginning:

'Oh, for that flame of living fire
  Which shone so bright in saints of old,
Which bade their souls to heaven aspire,
  Calm in distress, in danger bold.'

While singing the last stanza the Spirit of God was greatly manifested. Brother Dake requested that we repeat the stanza, which we did several times with telling effect. He finally closed the Bible and said: 'I can not get around that. This is my text, 'Remember, Lord, the ancient days.' He began to speak on the baptism of the Holy Ghost as lived and preached by the fathers. He made plain the hindrances in the way of receiving this primitive power.

"As he was closing his sermon the power of God came upon him in a wonderful manner which caused him to leap for joy. He said: 'I suppose I have lost my reputation as a preacher by leaving my text, but I had no reputation when I came.' But while he did leave his text and

followed the Spirit it was a wonderful sermon. He invited seekers to come to the altar and the scene that followed is indescribable. Sinners and backsliders were
crying for mercy, while the saints were pleading for the
baptism of fire. The meeting lasted until about midnight.
Some were slain by the power of God, while others sang
and prayed with those who were seeking.

"God was present in every meeting in saving power.
Among our brother's last words to the writer as we parted
at the depot, to meet no more on earth, were these (calling me by my first name as he always did): 'Horace,
PRAY, Pray, you can pray a hole through anything.'
Thus he spoke from his own personal experience. Here
he had found the secret of power."

FROM S. K. WHEATLAKE

I was well acquainted with the late Rev. V. A. Dake
in the latter years of his life and was associated with
him in several camp-meetings. He was a man of rare
qualities in many respects, but the greatest thing in his
life and what attracted my attention the most and drew
me to him was the deep spirit of devotion to God and His
work. He was profoundly spiritual and seemed to live in
the very atmosphere of heaven itself. To all appearance
he was in constant communion with God.

I first met him at the dedication of a church at Bliss-
field, Michigan, and was in his presence only a short time
when I sensed the fact that I was with a man who lived
very near to God and that he was moving within the
limits of a circle much nearer the Lord than I was, though
at that time I was in the enjoyment of a clean heart. In
less than an hour after meeting him I retired to a grove
near by and asked the Lord to help me into a deeper experience in the things of grace. Several have since told
me that his presence and spirit had the same effect on

them.   His very presence at times would make men think
about God and their own condition.   So great was his love
for God and His cause that at times it seemed to me that
his spirit of sacrifice and self-denial knew no bounds, for
with him God and His work was second to nothing on
earth and souls must be saved, if need be, at the loss of
all else.   He seemed to live constantly under a burden for
the lost, and I have known him to pray and weep for
hours over their lost condition.

He was a natural-born commander, and his tact and
great personality in connection with his almost intuitive
knowledge of human nature well adapted him as a leader
among men.   He possessed a faculty for prompting men to
action that I often righteously coveted.   At times his
tactics were rather peculiar and surprising, but as a rule
they terminated in victory.   I was at one time preaching
at a camp-meeting while he was seated in the stand.   Just
as I was ending up one of the divisions of my sermon he
suddenly sprang to his feet, and shouted, "Wait a minute,"
and took up the subject where I had left it and with great
power proceeded to open it up.   In a short time he paused
and said to me, "Go ahead."   I then announced my second
division and once more he took it up, and so on until the
sermon was finished.   Seeing that the hand of the Lord
was on him for that occasion, I did but little more than
announce my divisions while he preached the sermon.
Suffice it to say that doubly arranged sermon ended in
one of the most remarkable displays of divine power that
I ever witnessed.   Preachers fell in the stand and the
saints went down in the congregation and sinners came
screaming to the altar until three long altars were full
of them.   God often led him in such peculiar ways.   He
was far above the ordinary as a preacher.   As such he was
homiletic and made use of a great many telling illustra-
tions.   I have heard him preach some of the most unearthly sermons I ever heard.   At times his flights of elo-

quence and oratory were sublime. His descriptive powers were great and they enabled him to give some very vivid portrayals of sin in the hearts, lives, and homes of men. His word-pictures of hell and heaven were at times both terrific and beautiful. With the rest of mortals he had his infirmities and made some mistakes, but "he was a good man and full of the Holy Ghost." I am a better man to-day because of the life of V. A. Dake.

FROM J. BAKER

I was intimately acquainted with Rev. V. A. Dake. I sold him the first tent he used when he commenced his Pentecost work in Michigan. We gave him and his Bands the right of way on all of my circuits. At one time we had three Bands on one circuit. He was a welcome guest at our home, where he loved to come in times of trial and persecution. We ate, slept and rode together and I found him to be the most devoted, self-denying, careful, holy man I ever met, and a powerful preacher. I have seen a whole camp-meeting moved as with a cyclone and run to the altar under his powerful exhortation. The influence of his work will last as long as time, both in Michigan and other states. His zeal for the lost consumed his physical life. Had he been more considerate of his health, he doubtless would still be with us. His long fasts and sleepless nights spent in railroad stations to save money to carry on his work were too much for even his strong constitution. There are so many of the other class that the Lord will excuse him. Peace be to his memory, his "works do follow him."

FROM MRS. H. A. COON

To-day I received a request from Mrs. Ida Dake Parsons. It brings tears and rejoicing, for since the good

man died and was buried by the seaside, I have often wondered how his wife could keep still. It is with difficulty
that I have refrained from taking the pen in his behalf
in the years that have elapsed since that sad day, and
have wondered that no one did so.

Most of the pilgrims around Chicago went to "farewell" Rev. V. A. Dake when he departed for Africa. I
was in the home of Brother and Sister Gates, and they,
wondering that I did not prepare to go, said, "Mother,
are you not going?" "No, I can not." I had told him if
he went it would be farewell forever, as he would never
return. With surprise he answered, "Auntie, I'm coming
back." "No, Vivian, it is good-by till the judgment."
We were both sad. Three little shells are all I have to
remind me of his arrival there.

I have known him from his boyhood, and all the way
have known him to admire him. I was always glad to put
him in a room in my home when he came to Marengo;
often reminded him that he did not take food enough, as
he ate at the most times but twice a day, fasted regularly
three times a week and sometimes days at a time. He
made it a rule to spend one night each week in an all
night of prayer. He would pray in the barn, or coal house,
or cellar, or behind a tree, rather than be hindered.

He carried a constant burden for the lost; thought
nothing of laboring all night in prayer with a backslidden
preacher or worker, and would hold on to them as long as
hope remained.

Once in my house I went into the parlor and found him
at 2 o'clock in the morning on his knees asleep. Worn out
by burdens and fasting and constantly in meeting tired
nature had succumbed. I implored him to retire. In his
characteristic, meek manner, he said, "I will do better,
Auntie." What an example to those at ease in Zion. He
came with his Band to hold meetings in the Marengo
church. There was a standstill in the services and as we

talked it over together, I questioned them closely. It was a serious time. He was the first to fall on his face, saying, "I am to blame." Not a bite of food, but with unearthly groans he rolled on the floor crying out against the uncleanness of his heart and praying for deliverance. He refused to preach again until the cleansing power came. The glory filled him, the fire burned, and V. A. Dake was ever after a terror to the carnal professor and evil-doer.

He would write me to come to a meeting and as soon as I got there would appoint a close class for preachers and workers. Then he would get down on his face and groan. This often occurred, especially at his large gatherings.

He always preached the cleanest cut Bible truth, and held himself to the same line. I once remarked that if he knew of any one who could preach him under conviction that he would walk fifty miles, if necessary, to hear him.

His life passion was for souls. I never have known one so good, so true, so straight-forward, so plain, in fact, he was one the most like Jesus that I ever knew. His converts were clean, radical and fiery and so unlike the world in appearance that no one was left to guess which side they were on.

He was a strong advocate and preacher of entire sanctification. His teachings on this subject were deep and thorough. His converts never had any cause to fear that they had been skimmed over.

God called him to the special work of getting young converts to work and raising up Bands of young men and women and training them to that end. There never have been known any more self-denying, self-sacrificing young people than they, as they went singing, shouting and weeping on street corners, in dirty halls and even in prison for Jesus' sake. They were invincible for God as long as their leader lived, and were used of God in raising up societies and erecting many of our churches. But I must not close this sketch without speaking of the humility which always characterized our brother, also his loyalty to his church. At one time when some difference arose at conference, he remarked that if the church turned him out he would go to May street, Chicago, and join on probation.

He was a wise leader, careful almost to the extreme in the association of his Bands, carefully placing them and watching over all alike.

His courage knew no bounds. With a mighty faith in God and in his calling he went on through opposition, fiery trials and in poverty. He suffered, but he sang and shouted and loved his enemies. He lived as he wrote, "Only for souls my life work shall be, only for souls till death set me free," and died in the heat of battle, a victorious conqueror.

May God raise up many with like faith and courage to follow in his steps, is the prayer of your humble servant.

FROM REV. D. S. WARNER

My acquaintance with Vivian A. Dake began three years before he was graduated from Chili Seminary, and I was associated with him until he left the University of Rochester. I knew him when he was an unsaved young man. After his conversion he was intense in his religious life. He loved action. If any of his fellow students seemed to him to be sluggish spiritually, he was zealous in his efforts to stir them up. His love for souls was great. While he was in college, he gave much of his time to preaching at places near the city. Shortly after the opening of his junior year he became so restless and felt so strongly his duty to go to preaching the gospel, that he decided to leave the university immediately and enter the work. President Anderson and others tried to dissuade him from his purpose, but without avail. The last time I saw him was in the station in Rochester, where a number of his fellow students and friends bade him good-by as he took the train for the West

BY REV. H. D. F. GAFFIN

The memory of the just is blessed. At this writing, though fleeting time has chronicled decades since the subject of this tribute left the theater of earth's activities, answering the summons of Him who doeth all things well, still the memory of his holy ardor, earnest fervor, and untiring zeal for souls, lingers with us as sweet incense, warming our hearts and inspiring our zeal.

In our darkened vision and clouded judgment we say, what a loss to the church militant that one so young and who might have been so useful in life, should be taken away so early, yet to Him above must we look for a reason for it all, which we can not now understand, for Vivian, as we familiarly called him, seemed endowed and gifted above his fellows. As a herald of God, in pulpit, on the street, or in gospel song, he was without a peer.

It was my privilege to be associated with him in the work of God, he being our district elder in my early ministry. He always impressed me as one who knew Christ, and Him crucified, as a constant guide and companion.

His carriage was that of one who, knowing the terror of the Lord, would persuade men. Like Enoch he walked with God. Like Paul he could say, "The love of Christ constraineth me." His preaching and exhortations were in demonstration of the Spirit and with power. He spake as holy men of God when they were moved by the Holy Ghost.

Vivian was among the few men who in the gospel could be called all round men. Whether on his knees in secret prayer, at family devotions, at the penitent form directing souls to the Lamb of God; whether in exhortation, in sermon, or in song; whether in pulpit, or on the street, or in the leafy grove, or with pen in hand, he seemed always at his best, and under the anointing that abideth.

What he would have been, had God seen fit to spare him to the world, we know not. We know that the few years he lived as God's herald, he grew "as the lily, and cast forth his roots as Lebanon. His branches spread, and his beauty was as the olive tree."

We can not think of him as dead. No, he simply walked through the valley of the shadow of death. The setting sun on the closing day of earth's pilgrimage was the beginning of a new and brighter day to his ransomed soul.

Vivian is not dead. He has just gone before, and is waiting on the other side of the river of death. Sometime in the bright sunshine of the morning of eternal day we shall meet him, in the city which John saw, which had no need of the sun, neither of the moon to shine in it. There God shall wipe away all tears from our eyes, for there shall be no more death, neither sorrow nor crying.

BY REV. E. E. SHELHAMER

The writer hardly feels worthy to say anything about that holy, fearless, molder of men—Vivian A. Dake. If we were confined to one sentence in writing his epitaph, we should say, he was a *"flame of fire."* Perhaps this was why he preached and wrote so much about "kindling watch-fires" around the globe. Had he lived three-score years, doubtless he would have planted more mission stations throughout the world than any man since the days of St. Paul. As it was, we believe he set in motion and accomplished more at the age of thirty-seven, than most men do at twice that age.

He was not only radical on every issue, but unctuous as well. Like Gideon, God clothed himself with Vivian A. Dake. I have been in camp-meetings where things were grinding hard, and the coming of this man of God brought such courage and inspiration that immediately a wave of victory swept over the entire camp. His very tread seemed to make all hell uneasy. God used this spiritual general to lead the writer into a settled experience of holiness, after having professed the same a number of times. They said he was extreme. Perhaps he was in some things, but the writer would not ask a greater benediction than a double portion of that happy combination of zeal and humility, courage and carefulness, and above all the passion for souls which rested upon Vivian A. Dake. God raise up many others like unto him.

BY REV. D. G. SHEPARD

The Rev. Vivian A. Dake was a minister of great piety and devotion to God. He was a man of much prayer, and self-denial, especially in fasting and abstinence. The writer was associated with him in the work of the Lord in Iowa for a number of years, having been converted to God under his labors. He was our pastor for two years and afterwards was traveling chairman or district elder. We can truly say that we believe he was more often in secret prayer and that we found him in communion with God more frequently than any minister we were ever with during the same length of time. He was a man of great zeal and activity; always planning great things for God. The year the writer joined the Iowa conference of the Free Methodist church, Brother Dake had six appointments, and there were three local preachers from his circuit, who, having been recommended, united with the conference, all at one time.

Brother Dake was a *radical* preacher, and always endeavored to do *very thorough* work for God. His sermons were short and to the point. He was a minister who was not afraid to tell others in a kindly spirit what he saw wrong in them. Bywords and slang phrases would not

go unrebuked in his presence, especially when used by professors of religion. He was a man of very strong convictions and would always stand by them until convinced
that he was in the wrong.

The last year Brother Dake traveled the Walker, Iowa,
circuit, he and his wife lived in Walker, and I taught the
Walker school. Wife and I lived in the same house together with Brother and Sister Dake and all ate at the
same table. We found that Brother Dake closely and
profitably improved his time. It was during that winter
that he wrote the song, "We'll girdle the globe with salvation, and holiness unto the Lord." God used him in "dig-
ging out" a goodly number of preachers and getting them
into the regular work, some of them being spared to this
day.

FROM REV. A. C. SHOWERS

"Rev. V. A. Dake assisted me five weeks in meetings
at South Oil City, Pennsylvania. During this time, after
the first service, the altar was crowded with seekers. Such
a meeting was never witnessed by me in these parts. I
am safe in saying that hundreds never succeeded in gaining admittance to the church.

"The preaching was in demonstration of the Spirit and
with power. At one time the power of God so accompanied
his discourse as to almost overpower me. I suddenly arose
from my chair and sank again with an overwhelming sense
of the truth he presented. The saints in general were
quickened. Our work as a result took on a holier, more
spiritual character. The people of South Oil City will
never forget him. His ability as a preacher, while here,
was attributable not so much to sermonic distinctions as
to his unction and native force.

"He was never at a loss for imagery, forms of rhetoric,
words and expressions. His power as a speaker was large-

ly in his oratorical ability, which was not mechanical, but natural; he felt what he said. At one time in describing the scene of souls being lost he took his watch and in declaring that every time a watch ticked a soul dropped into eternity, we were so impressed that we could almost see and hear the thing itself. He dealt with men as for eternity.

"As regards his success in these meetings it can never be estimated. Now after two years we feel the effects. His personal piety and devotion were Scriptural in the extreme. He usually arose at five o'clock and sought God in prayer. He was frequently heard praying for 'Ida,' his beloved wife. Often he would drop everything and run to pray. He prayed one time for fifty dollars, which shortly came. His self-denial was remarkable. When he got any money he enclosed it in a letter to missions, or some other part of the field for God. He was wearing a worn-out overcoat while among us and being apprised of our intention to purchase a new one for him, he asked for the money, insisting that God's cause needed money more than he did the coat. I might rehearse ad infinitum, but desist to let the angels finish the eulogy."

CHAPTER VIII

MR. DAKE AS A PREACHER

Vivian A. Dake was a man of striking appearance, tall, well proportioned, with an open countenance, and a pleasant, though not handsome face. The expression in his mild, blue eyes and the lines of his mouth denoted determination and firmness of character. He was a man of vigorous mind, possessing great oratorical powers, a perfect command of language and unusual self-possession. A born speaker, he was at home in the pulpit. His countenance portrayed intelligence, affability and tenderness.

His conversational powers were remarkable and like his other powers were consecrated to the good of men and the glory of God. I never knew him, in any circle in which he might be found, to hold a conversation of any length which he did not turn into some channel for religious improvement. This was done in a manner so discreet, appropriate and gentle as not to awaken prejudice, but to conciliate and induce respect and good-will. It was not uncommon for him in mixed companies, when the secular concerns of the day were the theme of conversation, to interweave religious sentiments and reflections, so naturally deduced, so wisely stated, and so courteously and kindly applied, that even those who were generally most indifferent to religion could not but reverence it as it thus appeared in its venerable representative and minister.

We have seen him when he was transacting business with railroad officials and other business men, and noticed how his discretion and judgment were equalled only by his devotion to God. His words were so appropriate and well chosen at such times that he gained the respect of all, and succeeded in approaching them on the subject of eternal things, often conducting a conversation of some length, where ordinary men would have failed. His public and private prayers were always indicative of close communion with God, and characterized by a holy pathos and seriousness which were truly marvelous. Sometimes his discourses were rendered the more impressive by accompanying tears while the bliss of the redeemed or the despair of the wicked was vividly portrayed to his audience. His most striking characteristic in the pulpit was his extraordinary earnestness, which could not fail to attract attention, while his natural bearing, and easy, fearless manner, showed to all that he was master of the situation, and made one feel at home in his presence.

Another feature was his wonderful voice, rich, deep and powerful, yet under perfect control. We have stood on the outer limits of a congregation of several thousand people at a camp-meeting, and distinctly heard every word he said. He could whisper or thunder at will, swaying whole congregations by the modulations of his voice. His delivery was deliberate and emphatic, not generally loud or hurried, but when under special divine unction he took on strength and speed until a volume of burning truth was poured forth. Startling incidents from real life often figured in his sermons. Striking anecdotes, thrilling episodes, historical and imaginary, sat in his sermons like jewels in a crown, while poetry like a crystal stream sparkled through the green pastures of both his discourses and writings.

His apparently inexhaustible imagination and his happy art of word-painting made the imagery of his discourses appear as life. The influence of the latter was infused with his deep-toned piety, his self-sacrificing spirit and humble bearing, which could not fail to wield a molding influence for good. The mind was charmed by his zeal and eloquence, while the conscience was smitten by his pointed truths. He somehow possessed the power to take men by storm, and make his thoughts their thoughts, by clothing them in fire which burned into their souls in spite of prejudices. His descriptive powers were most marvelous. We have heard him describe, illustrate and denounce forms of wickedness and error in such terms that persons in the congregation, to him unknown, but who were known by others to be holding to the things condemned, have been seen to blush and hide their faces or leave the place in a rage.

His pen deserves some notice here. It was not the nice distinction contained in his writings which charmed, but his great personality which stood out in bold relief. His articles were written peculiarly for the hour, and accomplished the desired end. His personal characteristics were prominent in all his writings. His presence was felt in them, as that of a general is felt on the field of battle by his soldiers.

"Eloquence," wrote Dr. Stevens, "is the rarest, if not the greatest, power of genius, while pathos is the greatest, if not the rarest, power of eloquence." Mr. Dake possessed these oratorical qualities in a marked degree; but these fascinating gifts, of themselves, are often a greater curse than a blessing to their possessors. It is only when they are sanctified to the Master's use that they become a medium of blessing to mankind. We have no desire in this sketch to extol the accomplished orator, but rather the grace of God which made him what he was.

The flowery oratory, so prevalent in the pulpits of the nineteenth century, was never indulged in by him. The power of his eloquence lay in the earnestness and depth of his feelings. His style was peculiarly his own, earnest, terse and simple, while his language was better fitted for oral discourse than to be embodied in book form. Though this fault diminished his ability for didactic writing it added to his power as a speaker, in which capacity he excelled.

He depended for success upon the blessing of the Lord and not upon his own powers and exertions. To win souls was his only object and he concentrated all his powers to this end. He gave himself much to secret prayer and would come from those seasons of private devotion with a radiance on his face that gave a silent testimony to the divine unction on his soul. Oftentimes the burden of his prayer was for those who opposed him most. It was his custom to rise at an early hour to hold communion with God. A barn or shed was often the secluded spot where heaven came to greet his soul. At such times he would give vent to his pent-up feelings in such loud pleadings that many of the neighbors would be awakened, some of whom became greatly concerned about their souls and afterwards found peace with God. The best proof we can give of his private devotion was his great public success in soul-winning. In fact, he was not satisfied unless every moment of his time was spent in prayer, study, exhortation or counsel.

The extent and magnitude of his labors, wonderful though they were, scarcely equalled the intense earnestness with which they were performed. He deeply felt the import of the truths he preached, every look and gesture adding weight to his words. Thus prejudice vanished and truth conquered where defeat would have been unavoidable if presented with less fervency. Especially was this the case when dwelling on the terrors of the judgment or the responsibility of the sinner. Many times these impressive discourses were attended with such a burden for his lost hearers that it could not be expressed in words, but was seen in the tears which flowed freely down his face. For a time the sermon was stopped and the people were silent as death, held bound as by a spell, or else weeping out the pent-up feelings of their hearts.

His love for the lost constrained him to preach much
on the streets, in the city squares and in the parks. In
fact, he remained in few cities or towns any length of time
without singing up a congregation in the open air and
preaching to them. In these open-air meetings he was
right at home and his discourses were sometimes most
wonderful. As he looked into the faces of the neglected
and destitute ones who often formed part of his audience
and saw them as sheep without a shepherd he would at
times be melted to tears.

He seldom left an opportunity unimproved of awakening men to their awful danger. We have known him when
in a well-filled railroad coach, where all seemed more than
usually light and thoughtless, to rise with the gravity of a
judge and proceed with a brief and pointed discourse on
the shortness of time, the uncertainty of life, and the con-
sequent need of being at peace with God. Instantly the
frivolity would cease and the solemnity of eternity would
seem to take possession of the passengers. In these respects, too, he was an old-time Methodist. Would to God
we had many more such!

All his business transactions were prefaced and con-
cluded with prayer; and no task was so arduous but that
he kept his cheerful disposition through it. In fact, he
seemed to pursue his difficult and laborious course with as
much pleasure and zeal as men of the world do their sports.
Such cheerful dispositions, which grace can give to all,
the billows of opposition and persecution only tend to
lift heavenward, as the sea bird is borne higher by
the waves.

Like one who believed and felt what he preached, he
engaged in his work with enthusiasm, "in season and out
of season." His practical mind entertained no feeling of
fellowship for a merely cloistered theology. He exemplified the teaching and example of his Master, who "went
about doing good" to the souls and bodies of men; this

was his only ambition. His ideas of practical holiness were honored of God.

His increase of power with God brought a proportionate increase of opposition, coming often from those who should have been his friends. But this is no more than his divine Master and the holy men of all ages have received. Like Him, he was often "wounded in the house of his friends." The enemy had good reason to fear and oppose him, for wherever he labored the strongholds of darkness were shaken, and many of Satan's chief votaries were captured, saved by divine grace, and became devoted soldiers of Jesus.

The waves of opposition rolled high at times, yet the grace of God kept him triumphant through it all, and he was never found in a dejected mood. Music bubbled up spontaneously from his full heart. The following was written while passing through one of the heaviest afflictions of his life:

I WILL REJOICE

Though flocks and herds may perish,
  And fields may yield no store,
Though friends should all forsake me,
  I will rejoice evermore.

Though persecution cometh,
  A fierce and vengeful roar
Of hate, reproach and scorning,
  I will rejoice evermore.

Though feeble, faint and suffering,
  With burdens laden sore,
I'll shout till breaks the dawning;
  I will rejoice evermore.

For God Himself commandeth,
  I wait to hear no more,
But run to do His bidding;
  I will rejoice evermore.

Then on through every conflict,
    Till gleams the heavenly shore
And angels join the chorus,
    I will rejoice evermore.

History tells how Napoleon, when reaching a certain pass in the Alps, was brought to a halt, his general remarking that the ammunition wagons could not be drawn over so high a ridge. Bonaparte went to the leader of the band, found an inspiring march and ordered it played. The whole band struck up the animating music and under its inspiration the ammunition wagons went over the difficult place. Thus, through the influence of his cheerful musical nature, he was lifted over many a mountain of difficulty; and by his example others were often inspired to follow in his footsteps. He always met frowning adversity with a smile, as says Aristotle: "Suffering becomes beautiful when any one bears great calamities with cheerfulness, not through insensibility, but through greatness of mind."

OUTLINE OF SERMON PREACHED IN PRESBYTERIAN CHURCH, ATTICA, INDIANA

Text: "And the house, when it was in building, was built of stone made ready before it was brought thither: so that there was neither hammer nor ax nor any tool of iron heard in the house, while it was in building" (1 Kings 6:7). The stones for the temple had to be quarried. They were imprisoned by rubbish, bound fast by the earth. They must be digged out. These stones are not dead. They are "lively stones." But they can not stay in quarry, and at the same time undergo the process of preparation. Christ must have way, and with almighty power must excavate us. Some do not want to submit to the process. They do not want to give up progressive euchre parties, they do not want to abandon the theater and opera and the world. But all this rubbish must be wrenched away and from it all we must be quarried. Some of you well remember where and when Christ came with levers and pulleys and with grappling hooks and digged you from the "hole of the pit" and hewed you from the rigid rocks and tore you from the spirit-entombing rubbish of sin.

This a soul-harrowing process, this separation from the world. Colonel D—— was smitten with conviction from sin and fell into the hands of a Presbyterian pastor, a man of God, who dealt faithfully with souls. When he came inquiring, "What must I do to be saved?" he told him he probably had some preliminaries to attend to.

"You have dealt largely in horses, colonel, have you defrauded any one?"

"Yes, there is an honest old man over there, and I filched seventy dollars from him in a horse trade."

"Well," said the elder, "you must make restitution there before you can believe to the saving of your soul."

The colonel hurried away and confessed his wrong, handed over the seventy dollars and came back asking: "What must I do to be saved?" I thank God that the elder did not cry: "Believe, believe, believe and join our church, and give us your influence and your money," as some ministers do. He probed his conscience deeper still.

"Colonel, you have handled notes to a great extent. Have you wronged any one in that line?"

"Yes; I held a note against a penurious old deacon, who was proverbially stingy and grasping. He came and paid me one morning and I handed him the note. After he had gone I glanced across and saw he had left the note behind. I said, I will make that miserable old man pay for some of his scrapings. I filed the note away, and when I thought he had forgotten the affair, I dunned him for the money and confronted him with the note. In spite of all, he had it to pay."

"You must clear up that or you can never be saved."

Away he went confessing and restoring. He felt some easier after he had handed over the amount of the note, and came to the pastor's study with a lighter step, but only to be met with more soul-searching.

"Colonel, you have held many mortgages of late. Have you oppressed and robbed anybody in this business?"

"Yes, yes, an unfortunate man, in feeble health with a wife and family. I took advantage of a flaw and forced his property from him."

"You must right the wrong or lose your soul eternally."

Away he went and found a weary woman, weeping at her work, in a hut in which they had sought shelter. Want was staring all around. "Where is your husband?" he said.

"Oh, he is over yonder, trying the best he can to get something to keep the wolf from the door. He has a hard struggle and we are almost to the brink."

"Well, cheer up, and dry your tears," said he. "Here is seven hundred dollars I took from you, and here is my note for eight hundred dollars more that belongs to you."

Before he left that house God had shown Colonel D—— what he must do to be saved. No man can believe until he makes right every known wrong.

The next process is to bring the stones into line. This represents sanctification. You find the Word of God is very clear and explicit upon this doctrine; teaching emphatically that we are to be cleansed from carnal tempers, from unholy elements of nature after we are converted. Read the first epistle to the Thessalonians and see how very natural that is in setting forth the truth of holiness. You find it is addressed to those who are soundly converted. They were elected by the grace of God. "We give thanks to God always for you all, making mention of you in our prayers; remembering without ceasing your work of faith, and labor of love, and patience of hope in our Lord Jesus Christ, in the sight of God and our Father; knowing, brethren beloved, your election of God."

In the third chapter Paul prays, "And the Lord make you to increase and abound in love, one toward another, and toward all men, even as we do toward you: to the end He may stablish your hearts unblamable in holiness before God, even our Father." He is not praying for something that has been done or for something to be done for unconverted souls, nor for something that is impossible to have done now. And in the fifth chapter he is still praying for the same thing, and that it may be done now. We give you Scripture texts that need not the least twisting or turning to bring them to bear upon this subject. "And the very God of peace sanctify you wholly; and I pray God your whole spirit and soul and body be preserved blameless unto the coming of our Lord Jesus Christ. Faithful is He that calleth you, who also will do it."

This doctrine is not of man, but is taught in the wondrous words of the Son of God, when He said, "Thou shalt love the Lord thy God with all thy heart, and with all thy mind, and thy neighbor as thyself," and is taught in your Presbyterian catechism: "The chief end of man upon the earth is to glorify God, that he may enjoy Him forever." Amen.

Noiselessly, stone upon stone, grew this great temple of God, built of stones made ready before they were brought. "There was neither hammer, nor ax, nor any tool of iron heard in the house while it was building." So is the house on high built of "lively stones," "an holy priesthood," the eternal temple of our God. But the quarry is not a quiet place. There is heard the sound of hammers and chisels. There drills are ringing, and workmen shouting and running and sweating. There goes a blast, and there a great ledge of rock comes thundering down. The quarry is a place of business, and there is the noise

and whirl of eager activities, as souls are excavated and
fitted for the symmetries and the symphonies of heaven.
A man who had never heard a piano before was so thrilled
and enraptured with the wondrous melody that he started
off to find the piano factory, expecting there to be rav-
ished by the many, mingling strains of music. But he
found only the whirl and buzz of machinery, the rasping
sound of saws, the clatter of hammers, the patter of hurry-
ing feet, and dust, and din, and stroke, and shout, with
which the work went on. Wait a while; nor chide the din
and rush and shout; we are making pianos.

But these "lively stones" after they are brought into
line, are to be polished. A short time since they were
shapeless hard-heads or rough boulders of granite. You
can see your features reflect in the massive pillars that
rise in front of the court house in Chicago. God polishes
with life's tests and trials until His saints shine.

A chaplain in the war of the rebellion lay sick in the
far south, near unto death. No kind hand ministered to
him, except that of an old black woman. He complained
to her one day as she came, her black face beaming with
joy, into the tent, and bewailed his lonely and afflicted condition, far from wife and family and friends.

"You know nothing of such trials, Chloe, and so you
are cheerful and happy and shining with joy."

"I know nothing of trials, massa, do you say?"

And then she told him how her old master tore her darling children from her, one by one, and sold them into the
southern rice swamps to toil and die; and how at last he
sold her good, old husband who had loved her so long, and
she saw him driven off to rice swamps to die, and she never
saw her dear ones again, and in her old age her master
sold her to die in the same way; and as she talked on the
chaplain rose up and looked at her face that shone while
the tears streamed down her cheeks, and he cried out:

"Chloe, Chloe, how can you keep the joy beaming and glory shining under such sorrows?"

"Oh, massa, when I sees a dark storm gathering," said she, and she put her hand as if she saw some black cloud was coming into the tent, "then I just look round on the other side and there is Jesus, and it is all bright there."

"Among whom ye shine as lights in the world." Amen.

CHAPTER IX

THE WRITINGS OF MR. DAKE

The following stirring articles are from the pen of Mr. Dake, which have been taken from the *Free Methodist* and other religious journals.

PROHIBITION

Prohibition is God's method of dealing with sin, whether inherited or acquired; it is God's law. God does not prohibit great sins, and wink at small ones, popularly speaking. He condemns the sin, whether it manifests itself in a great or small degree. God does not demand moral purity of one, and a lower standard of another, because of circumstances or previous training. Neither does He demand holiness because of one's profession of the same, and regard with complacency a departure from the standard by one because he makes no profession. God has one law, one standard, and that affirmatively, purity; negatively, "prohibition." Men license sin in church and state; God licenses sin, never.

He is at eternal enmity with its every manifestation. Men soften the name. They say popularity, influence, respectability, self-interest are harmless amusements, necessary vices; God says they are sin. Men seek for the dividing line between sin and holiness, they seek long and earnestly through winding and devious ways, and appear with a smile of triumph in the church with flying banners inscribed, "Compromise;" in the state, "License." Sinai gathers blackness, as God's voice thunders in return, "Prohibition." Here is the "great gulf fixed." "Ye can not serve God and mammon" (Matt. 6:24). "He that committeth sin is of the devil" (1 John 3:8). If this is God's law in the church, it is God's law in the State, on all moral reforms. When the Republican party had for its motto, "The non-extension of slavery," license for sin—disaster followed disaster. There was first secession, then war and defeat. At Bull's Run, at Ball's Bluff, at Wilson's Creek, at Belmont, the Northern armies were defeated, and the blood of the bravest dyed the battle-fields. While "compromise" was the watchword, the star of the nation trembled in the balance, but when the Proclamation of Emancipation was heralded, it struck God's order—prohibition. Then came confidence, victory, triumph. In the temperance reform we have long been on the human order. Low license, high license, and local option are only so many temporizing methods, and bring defeat. We have had our "Ai's," our Waterloos, our Bull Runs, but we have had an "Achan in the camp." We were temporizing for the "Babylonish garment and the wedge of gold." Now we have struck God's line. Instead of devising human laws, we have accepted God's law—prohibition.

Mark the change! Confidence is with us, discouragement with our enemies. The *Champion,* the organ of the liquor interest of the Northwest, shrieks out like the wail of a lost spirit.

Once more we call your attention to our danger. There was mirth, rejoicing, carousing, and revelry in the dining hall of the Babylonian monarch, Belshazzar, when the mysterious hand traced on the wall in fiery characters the ominous words, "Mene, mene, tekel, upharsin." * * * Saloon-keepers, liquor dealers, brewers, distillers, beware. The muster of the prohibition hosts at the late election is your "mene, mene, tekel, upharsin." Rouse yourselves from the lethargy, fight for your rights, your business, for your homes.

Hallelujah! Victory is ours. God's order brings eternal victory. "Rouse, ye sleepy ones. To the ranks, ye stragglers." Do not be confused. Do not be deceived. This is God's order with sin, or with his arch servant, alcohol.

LOST SOULS

Lost souls! Can you get a faint idea of the measureless depth of meaning in the two small words? What oceans of tears! What overwhelming bursts of wailing and gnashing of teeth! What eternities of despair! Irredeemably lost! No chance for a light to shine out in their devil-begirt, furnace-heated, pall-shrouded, downward, outward, hellward pathway. Lost to heaven and hope! Lost! and no hope of ever being found. Not one dim, distant hope of ever being anything but more hopelessly, ruinously, despairingly lost, during all the eternities to come.

From woe to more woe; misery to worse misery; ever, always lost! Lost, because they would be lost. Lost, while their bosom friend was found. Lost, while Jesus was speeding them, and found them, lost; but they would not be found. They might have been found, but would not. They gained the world and lost their souls. They gained the shadow and lost the substance; gained the briers and lost the flowers; gained famine, and lost plenty; gained foes, and lost a Friend; gained eternal damnation, and lost eternal life.

Lost amid the outer darkness! Lost in the smoke of torment! Lost in the lake of fire and brimstone! Lost amid the howling of myriads of tormenting devils, the shrieks of the damned; "an horrible tempest," ten thousand thunders! Lost! Lost!! Lost!!! The bells of eternity are tolling the requiem. Time warns you. The Bible warns you. The judgments and providences of God warn you. The Spirit warns you. Shall you and your loved ones be lost? Decide now while Jesus calls, or you are lost.

A WHOLE LIFE-TIME LOST

How? To whom do your refer? Oh! I know. You mean drunkards, adulterers, gamblers, prostitutes, murderers and all such vile sinners. My title is true of them, but I have in my mind quite a different class. I see before me pilgrims who used to be full of the fire. They never knew what it was to let a day pass over their heads without a special blessing. They were at all the camp-meetings and general gatherings, and their hearty, Holy Ghost-inspired amens were refreshing to saints and terrifying to sinners in Zion. They were very poor in this world's goods, but rich in faith. They moved out on the prairie on a government claim. They honored God and He smiled on them and prospered them.

Then came a change. "The care of this world, and the deceitfulness of riches, choke the word." They were just as straight outwardly. They would shout amen to the echo, when any one preached on Masonry, tobacco or dress, or glorified the church; but let them touch on covetousness, loss of fire, or power, and their heads were down. They gave less out of their abundance than formerly out of their poverty, and grumbled more over what they did give. They worked harder and longer hours to lay up another dollar than they did before for bread to eat.

The end came. They went to meet God, a just God, perhaps unconscious—doped and benumbed with doctors' drugs. The will was read, and all of their thousands went into the hands of truth-hating, holiness-fighting, world-loving, unsaved children.

A life-time was lost, for this money represented the

toll of their lives. They had turned over the whole of their life-time's hard work to the enemies of God. What did we say of the nation or man who furnished the rebels money with which to fight the government? How does God regard those who put all their money into the hands of His enemies? But you say, "Mine are good children." They are, if unsaved, the enemies of God; and you are thus putting into their hands the means with which to fight God. Then that money may build them up in arrogance and pride and damn their souls.

Sad for you, if at the judgment you should find that you had not only thrown away the result of your whole life, furnished the enemies of God means to push their fight against their God, but had been the means of the utter damnation of your own children.

Brethren, call a halt. Look over the field. Hear the call of God. What are you accumulating money for? Are you not handling God's money? "Will a man rob God?" Will you give to the unsaved (and your children are no better than any other sinners in God's eyes, however dear to you) the means that belong to God? Rob God of His own, and lose the rich reward that might be yours, as a faithful steward? "Lay not up for yourselves treasures upon earth." "Take heed, and beware of covetousness."

Oh! the unbuilt churches, the weeping heathen, the suffering poor, the needy missionaries, the millions dropping to hell, and you laying up your thousands for the enemies of God! Professedly, you are for God, but covertly you are supplying the enemy with the sinews of war.

God arouse you. Covetousness will be your ruin. You will go into hell together with those whom you thus strengthen in iniquity. Hearken! Live for God. Make your money preach for God while you live. You will not have much left when you die; and what you do have, you will safely secure to its rightful possessor—the jealous and covenant-keeping God.

CONSTANT VICTORY

God wants to give you constant victory. Has He not told you to "rejoice evermore"? "This is the victory that overcometh the world, even our faith." Have you constant faith? Then you have constant victory also. All discouragements are from the devil, all victories from God. How do you get discouraged? By testimony to the author of all discouragements—the devil. But are not some things discouraging? God says, "And we know that all things work together for good to them that love God." Do not listen to the devil one moment. If he gets your ear a moment, he has a chance to overcome you. Ear-gate is the most important entrance to Man-soul.

The serpent gained the first victory over Eve when she stopped to listen to his seductive voice. (See Gen. 3:1.) Thus he secures every advantage. Keep your ears so attuned to the voice of God that you will detect the voice of a stranger (the devil) and follow him not. Are your circumstances hard? Begin to rejoice that they are not more severe. This is one of God's ways to purge you. "Rejoice, and leap for joy." Does your present sphere of labor please God? Then you should be satisfied to please the King of heaven. Is God pleased with you in your self-denial and sufferings? This should cause you more rejoicing than to be called to the rest of heaven, or to take an archangel's trumpet. Amid all that was brought to bear upon the Apostle Paul, the only thing that the devil could get out of him was rejoicing in victories.

Beaten, stoned, imprisoned, bruised, chased from city to city, shipwrecked, hungry, and thirsty, even near to death, yet hear him close up with these remarkable words, "Therefore, I take pleasure in infirmities, in reproaches, in necessities, in persecutions, in distresses, for Christ's sake." (See 1 Cor. 11:12.) O brother, magnify the grace of God! "The humble shall hear thereof, and be glad." "Let all things be done without murmurings."

"Be content with such things as ye have; for He hath said, I will never leave thee, nor forsake thee." You can rejoice in the victory in the time of sorrow and mourning. Peter and John came to the sepulchre, looked in, went in, saw nothing but the linen clothing. Then they, discouraged, went home. Mary stood at the door, at the place of mourning, until (John 20: 12) first she saw a heavenly scene, two angels in white; then she continued there until she saw (verses 14, 18) Jesus.

Rejoice! What in? My circumstances are so discouraging. "Rejoice in the Lord alway: and again I say rejoice!" "Rejoicing in hope of the glory of God." "I will joy in the God of my salvation." "I am the Lord, I change not," so that we can joy in Him "yesterday, and to-day and forever" the same. "The water that I shall give him shall be in him a well of water springing up into everlasting life." This last verse will show you the reason you fail, get discouraged, get blue, and can not keep where God's word gives you the privilege. You lack the overflowing wells. Dig deep. You can have it. Do not stop until you find it. "Chase the self-love through all your heart, through all its latent mazes there." With the death of the old nature, and the incoming of the all-cleansing blood, you will find "what your soul so long has craved." Do you profess holiness, and yet this is not your experience? You are deceived. Get the experience, and the victory is yours, "For thus saith the Lord."

SLOTHFULNESS—NO. 1

Well did President Edwards say, "Slothfulness in the cause of God is as damning as open rebellion."

The meager work of nineteenth-century professors dwindles down to an almost invisible point, when compared with the pressed and crowded lives of the primitive

Christians. "Always abounding in the work of the Lord," was the measure of their work. "Redeeming the time because the days are evil," and working while 'tis day, "for the night cometh when no man can work," gave them no time for idling.

Brother preacher, how will you be able to meet God in peace, amid the shrieks and cries of a sinking world, when your secret place has become a form, and is hurriedly passed over or altogether neglected? When the Holy Bible has lost its sweetness? When the unctuous spirit has left your prayer and pulpit exercises, and when you have lost your feeling for perishing souls to the degree that you can hold from two to six weeks of extra revival effort, visit your members but little, unless starved to it, and the unsaved families around you seldom if ever, spend your time in your study or on your easy couch, or busied in temporalities, and come to conference full of complaints at your salary and hard fare? Oh, what a sight! Little, two-by-four circuits, and preachers creeping around in their little ruts, and a world, from the borders of their own narrow sphere clear to Africa, holding up its hands and crying, "No man cares for my soul."

Are our carriages too fine and our horses too sleek to brave the hardships with the "sheepskin and goatskin" company? I tell you the gallant circuit riders of seventy-five years ago, with their saddle-bags and 200-mile circuits, their shining faces and triumphant shouts, put us to the blush.

How many will be damned, not because they were not orthodox or radical, but because they were slothful in the cause of God? O brother, what avails your boasted orthodoxy or radicalism if your circuits run down on your hands? If your efforts for the lost are spasmodic and unfruitful, and if your report to conference and at the throne is, "No success this year"? Away with such radicalism! Give us a radicalism on fire with melting love for lost men, that will "leap over walls," "run through troops," brave "horrible pits of miry clay," search Gadara's tombs, and run to the crumbling edge of the pit to "snatch men out of the fire." Give us a ministry that have no idle moments; that are pressed with work like a cart pressed with sheaves; that live in the sight of the judgment; that walk head and shoulders in eternity; that have their "conversation in heaven;" that "redeem the time," "abound in the work of the Lord;" "whose heads are waters and their eyes a fountain of tears;" and who "see the travail of their souls and are satisfied," and Pentecost will come again, our work-day will last until rest day, and "we shall come rejoicing, bringing in the sheaves." God speed the day!

SLOTHFULNESS—NO. 2

"Woe unto them that are at ease in Zion."

Brother layman, please look at that verse of scripture thoughtfully, honestly. You feel while thinking it over an internal satisfaction, guaranteed by the Holy Ghost, that you are "instant in season and out of season," or the woe is upon you. You love a live, energetic preacher, who lives on the move, but how is your spiritual pulse? Do you crawl out of bed two or three hours later on Sabbath morning than you do on week-day mornings?

Do you secretly wish you could stay at home and take a nap, instead of going to class and preaching? Do you settle yourself into a comfortable corner of the seat and nod, sleep, and mayhap snore, while the preacher labors to point out the way of life? Do you go to bed without the family altar at night? Are you too spiritually feeble to attend the week-night prayer-meetings? Too weak to "visit the fatherless, the widows in their affliction," and the unsaved in their lost condition, to comfort and to warn? Are you too far gone to fast even once in three

months at the quarterly fast appointed by the Discipline?
O brother, what would eternity reveal to your gaze?
You used to be very earnest in the observance of all these
duties, and self-denial and cross-bearing were your delight,
but you began to think there was no need of wearing out
one's self by so much work for God, and forgot that God
said, "He that loveth his life shall lose it." So your spiritual decline has been rapid. Damning sloth has entered
your spiritual veins, and you are just becoming palsied.
Oh, awake, in Jesus' name!

"Work while the day lasts." Bend all your energies
in hope of winning souls for heaven. The harvest is
great; the fields are ripe. Harvest time will soon be over,
and shall your work remain undone?

Will it pay thus to trifle this brief life away? There
will come a day when your slothfulness will vanish as the
morning dew, and you will be keenly alive to the fact that
your awakening is too late. Time past! Earth receding!
Work-day forever gone by, and now all your misspent time
to meet at the judgment.

MY BROTHER'S KEEPER

The Sabbath question is one of the great problems of
the day. Thousands of men are employed on the railroads,
in the postal and telegraphic services, telephone and
manufacturing companies, who know no Sabbath. The
open doors of the saloon conspire to change the Sabbath
from the Lord's day to a day of darkness.

The men who work on the Sabbath do so largely against
their will. Mr. Grinnell, of Iowa, said, at Farwell Hall,
that at one time he had 1,000 men working under him on
the railroad, and he took the mind of 700 of them on keeping the Sabbath, and of the 700 all voted to rest on the
Sabbath except sixteen. The saddest feature of the matter

is that professed Christians aid and abet this work. They get their mails, ride on the cars, take Sunday newspapers, and buy milk on the Lord's day.

Our holiness work, and Free Methodism especially, stands in the van of many reforms; but many good people among us ride on the Sunday street cars. Is this consistent? Many to whom we talk loudly of "outward adorning" and "secrecy" could not be persuaded to ride on the cars on the Sabbath. Brother, sister, could you reprove that street car conductor for Sabbath-breaking and non-attendance at church while you ride with him on the holy day? Do I hear you answer, "Am I my brother's keeper?" Yes; and thousands of down-trodden men who have no Sabbath, and who feel compelled to work on the Sabbath to support their children, will cry against you at the judgment, and their cry will enter into the ear of the Lord of Sabaoth. The excuses and pleas are only types of those used by the dram or tobacco seller, or the violator of any of God's laws. One says: "I could not attend church." Then stay at home, and do missionary work among your neighbors. Another says, "Is it worse than to drive my horse?" Vastly. You are aiding by your influence a giant Sabbath-breaking corporation. Another says, "I must ride or I can not do as much good." God's woe is pronounced against those who say, "Let us do evil, that good may come, whose damnation is just" (Rom. 3:8).

A young man in the employ of a certain railroad was one day ordered by the superintendent to take a train out on the Sabbath day. He replied, "I have been brought up to revere the Sabbath, and I can not go." The superintendent said, "Then you forfeit your place." Rather than lose his place he obeyed. While getting his train ready he fell under the wheels and was mortally injured. While he was lying in the agonies of death that superintendent came to him and said, "Poor fellow! Don't worry. I'll pay for your coffin and funeral expenses." "Yes," said the dying man, as he turned his glassy eyes full on the superintendent, "but who'll pay for my soul?"

HAVE YOU LOST YOUR FIRST LOVE?

This question is first to the "angel of the church," or the pastor, and then to the individual members of the church. The increasing danger in this direction lies in the fact that the church and the world are every day becoming more alike. The old landmarks are being removed, and a tide of popularity is overwhelming even the "little one" that God raised up to spread scriptural holiness over these lands.

Free Methodists, do you know your danger? Do you know that many preachers and people have lost their first love? They are putting the head for the heart experience. Growing in knowledge, they imagine it to be grace. If you have lost your first love, where is the power that characterized your early experience; the earnest fervor of soul, the intense yearning and longing after the perishing around you, the tender conscience, the careful listening for the whispering of the Spirit, the soul satisfying communings with your Redeemer, the wrestling and prevailing, as heaven crowned you a prince, saying, "As a prince hast thou power with God and with men, and hast prevailed"? Is not this the experience of the past? And you have experience and knowledge now instead? Will you hearken to the voice of God, "I have somewhat against thee because thou hast left thy first love"? You have gotten over the weakness and childishness of your early experience; yes, and with it your first love, your power, your success. O trumpet of God's truth, blow a blast in our ears and rouse our sleepy souls!

My brother, my sister, is your experience back of the experience of the past? "Remember from whence thou art fallen!" Remember how you loved your secret place—now such a weary task. How the means of grace were your delight, and you could suffer any denial, or walk weary miles "to sit in the heavenly places," away from which you can now stay by silencing your conscience with, "I pray thee, have me excused." Remember how you watched your words, how jesting, or idle words, or evil-speaking, grieved your very soul; but now you can spend the precious, heaven-born, eternity-freighted minutes in serving Satan in your words. Remember the power of God that brought a silent awe, or a shout of victory as the people of God prevailed together! Now how we frown down such as fanaticism or excitement, and thank God that we are in a higher state of knowledge! O soul of mine, weep for the "daughter of my people"! Oh, remember, remember from whence thou art fallen! Fashionable, world-baptized, "believe-you've-got-it" holiness is carrying us away like a mighty torrent. Instead of the death groans as the soul dies out to the world or to the carnal mind, you hear the mischievous whisper, "Believe you've got it." (Do you see? Do you acknowledge?) "Repent, and do the first works; or else I will come unto thee quickly, and will remove thy candlestick out of his place, except thou repent." This is the only way back to first love. Promises, good resolutions, all, all fail. Repent! Repent! Confess thy fall, and God will repent Himself, and our "candlestick" will remain.

Oh, you that cry, "Peace, peace, when there is no peace," forbear! If you will not repent yourself, let the people repent. My fathers, my brethren, my children, the old track is the only track. O rugged, bloody "cross of the Crucified One," we will bear thy reproach. Let the trumpet thunder anew along the line, "No quarters to sin." Let us go back to our ancient plainness, simplicity, humility, purity, watchfulness and power. "I can not hold my peace, because thou hast heard, O my soul, the sound

of war." "I have set watchmen on thy walls, O Jerusalem,
that shall never hold their peace day nor night." "Cry
aloud, spare not, lift up thy voice like a trumpet, and show
thy people their transgressions, and the house of Jacob
(Free Methodists) their sins."

THE DIVIDING LINE—NO. 1

We are in danger of being swamped by the modern
holiness movement. Holiness is becoming popular, and
the proud, worldly, and aristocratic of the day are talking
about being saved from all sin, while they still live in and
for the world. How shall we avoid the threatened danger?
By insisting more thoroughly on separation from the
world as necessary to pardon. If one has not the light
then let the light shine. We are becoming too weak-
kneed on this, and are allowing to ourselves the possibility
of some having the world, and yet being saved. We may
allow the possibility of individuals not having light, but
that does not release us of the responsibility of letting
the light shine upon them, nor them from walking in it
when it does shine.

Justified persons do not love the world, and if they see
anything about them in appearance worldly, they gladly
get rid of it, when pointed out. "If any man love the
world, the love of the Father is not in him." Show the
people that God demands separation. If justified, they
gladly receive the light. If they refuse the light, this is
their condemnation, that "men loved darkness rather than
light, because their deeds were evil."

Holding steadily to separation from the world will do
much to turn back the tide of popular holiness. The
danger here lies in our granting the fact that after light
shines those outwardly worldly can continue in a justified
and even a sanctified state without walking in the same.

We do not grant this in our theology or preaching; but like many popular teachers are we not beginning to fearfully fail in the enforcement of the same? When the signs of worldliness do not stir us to vigilance it is because we are backsliding ourselves. Have you done your duty here, my brother? Sound an alarm in God's holy mountain.

Worldliness is on the increase, and we shall be swamped unless we take timely warning. Which side of the line are you on, brother? "Ye can not serve God and mammon."

THE DIVIDING LINE—NO. 2

We shall avoid the threatened danger from the popular holiness movement by insisting on death to the carnal mind. While this is in our theology, it is almost entirely neglected in our altar work. The generalization of the modern teacher is overwhelming us. Consecrate all and then believe, in general terms, is all we hear insisted on. The Bible teaches a death, a crucifixion of the "old man." This is the place to bring in the conflict. Begin to talk death to carnality, and there is a stir among carnal holiness professors.

Around our altars twenty years ago we used to hear the cries, "Let me die," "Crucify the old nature," and the groans of the dying were heard. But we have holiness made easy in these days. The trouble is, the seeker does not see the blackness of inbred sin. He does not realize the awful nature that dwells within.

The body of sin contains all the elements of iniquity. When the seeker gets his eyes open to it, then comes in the agony of death. I believe in every case there will be agony, and a sense of the death throes, if the individual goes through on the line shown by the Apostle Paul in Romans 6:6.

No doubt there are thousands deceived to-day who

have gone through with the intellectual formula. It is, "I consecrate all and put it on the altar. The altar sanctifies the gift. I believe God's words and I am now sanctified." The poor soul often finds pride, envy, jealousy, touchiness, peevishness, impatience, stubbornness, love of flattery, desire for place, lustfulness, evil thoughts, evil surmisings, etc., in his heart, but calls it temptation, goes through with his formula, and goes on saying to himself, "There isn't as much in holiness as I thought, but I must believe and not dishonor God." Oh! bring your "old man" to the cross. He hates the cross, but bring him to it. Now not in theory, if you please, but confess your carnality to God. Look at the blackness until you realize it. Cry out to God, "Let me die." Don't waver nor let any dauber with untempered mortar divide your mind. It shall be done. You will know when you have gone through the death throes. Consecration will walk hand in hand with the death agony; and when your "old man" is dead, your consecration will be complete. Hallelujah! Then faith will spring up and grasp God easily, naturally. Amen. God bless you. Go to the rock.

POWERLESS PREACHERS

Are you inquiring why you do not succeed in your work and why the church is, as a whole, retrograding? Let God answer you: "I have somewhat against thee because thou hast left thy first love" (Rev. 3:4). Brother, answer the following questions as for eternity.

First, Have you not lost your unction in the pulpit?

Second, Have you not lost your longing for secret prayers?

Third, Have you not lost your burning zeal for searching of the Word of God?

Fourth, Have you not lost your burning zeal for perishing souls?

Fifth, Have you not lost the fulness of the Spirit, so
that you must stop and reason with yourself to convince
yourself that you are really what you say you are? If so,
will you answer at the bar of your conscience, with the
light of God shining upon you, this question, What have
you left? Oh! do not lay the lack of success and the
dying out of the work to the extravagancies of a few
anointed ones, or to the "new movements" springing up
among us. It is the lack of the Holy Ghost in your
heart and life. Thank God, some are seeing it. Six or
eight preachers in the last three or four weeks have confessed their heart backslidings and have found the old joy
and power. A true revival must begin in the pulpit.
Don't begin to say, "Well, but I am true to the issues." It
is this dry hammering upon "issues" that kills. Come,
brother, get the Spirit on you or God will remove your
candlestick out of its place. I feel divinely commissioned
to sound an alarm in your holy mountain. We are burdened with an unbaptized ministry, and we shall surely
fail to do the work God has given in our hands unless the
ten days' prayer-meeting shall begin with every dry and
formal preacher.

Then shall we go forth "clear as the sun, fair as the
moon, and terrible as an army with banners." We believe
in an unctuous straightness. "The letter killeth, but the
Spirit giveth life." "Who maketh his * * * ministers a
flame of fire." "Tarry ye at Jerusalem until ye are endued
with power from on high." Let the Pentecost begin.

"Flame of fire" is the New Testament definition of a
minister. "Who maketh his * * * ministers a flame of
fire.' How filled this figure is with meaning and earnestness. No idleness; grasping on to everything, inflammable,
winding its fiery arms around everything in its pathway.
The flame of fire rushes on. So God's minister has no time

for idleness. He is a flame of fire for the salvation of men. His body may be consumed, his all, it matters not. The zeal of God's house eats him up. He is in an agony for the souls of men. He cries out, "Give me souls or I die." He has no time for mirth, trifling, vain talk and chitchat, mere visiting or whiling away of time. He has no time to go over to Sister C's to have a good, social visit. He is aflame with love and zeal.

God pity those who call themselves ministers and have no more fire about them than Arctic icebergs. They shiver at the very thought of fire, and have a moral chill if a flame of fire comes into their vicinity. Such know nothing about the life more abundant. They live where the forms of life are very low and small. The faithful minister has "a wall of fire round about" him. He lives in the torrid zone where the forms of life are very numerous and luxuriant.

He partakes of the nature of the wall around him until he himself becomes a flame of fire. He is full of life, has "life more abundantly." He runs, crying, "Life, life, eternal life." A flame of fire consumes everything inflammable, pleasant, beautiful things, or disagreeable.

The man of God arises in his might against all sin. He reproves the class leader for shaving and blacking his boots on the Sabbath, the class leader's wife for buying milk or riding on the street cars on the Sabbath day, and the man who gives the most toward his support for breaking his contract with the unsaved wheat buyers; reproves his members for laying up treasures on earth, for making a god of their stomachs, for getting the Sunday headache and the prayer-meeting rheumatism, for lightness and trifling, for whispering and backbiting, for worldliness and compromise.

He reproves men for building fine houses to please the lust of their eyes; for buying rich furniture; for spreading sumptuous tables and laying up money for unsaved children to damn their souls with, while God's cause is moving slowly for lack of means and thousands are rushing to hell. He fears no man; he fears God. He is "so dead that no desire doth rise to appear good, or great, or wise, in any but his Savior's eyes." Brother ministers, are you a flame of fire?

While God's ministers are to be a flame of fire, all of God's people are to have a WALL OF FIRE. "I will be to them a wall of fire round about and the glory in the midst of them." The fiery wall of the saint is first a defense. As wild beasts hate and fear natural fire, so devils and worldly-minded men hate this fire (divine power). The wall of fire is the security of God's saints. Within it they are safe. Then it is a separation. The world is divided from the saint by a wall they can not pass over. If they attempt to come with worldly, combustible trash, it takes fire and adds to the flame.

Hence the world keeps far off from the saint. A mighty gulf is fixed between. They can not stand the fire. A man surrounded by this wall never testifies: "I have such hard work to keep the world away from me," for the world keeps its distance. The wall of fire chases away the darkness. On the face of the saint the heavenly glow radiates, caused by such a divine surrounding, and chases all the dark clouds away.

The pathway is plain, enlightened by the light of the Lord. They do not walk in darkness but have the light of life. It is accompanied by the glory. Where the wall of fire is, there the glory is in the midst. If you have not the glory you have not the wall of fire; hence no defense, no separation, no light. But the glory is the inner accompaniment of the fiery wall. God's saints are full of glory, because full of God, filled with the Spirit. Do you live for God? Are you all on fire? Wake up! The alarm is being sounded. No soldiers in heaven's army but those who have the "glory for a defense."

ALWAYS ABOUNDING

None but the most important work could call forth
such an expression as the above. "Always," referring to
the extent of time, and "abounding" to the extent of effort.
How many content themselves with spasmodic effort.
Sunday religion, protracted-meeting earnestness, is the
rule, while the exception is to find one always "in season
and out of season" earnestly preparing for eternity and
warning the lost. This does not give any time for pleasure-
seeking and worldly recreation. It monopolizes every
moment, day and night, winter and summer, seed-time and
harvest, to God's glory.

Men act as though they could give a certain portion
of their time to God's cause and then they could do as they
please with the balance. Oh, what a sight to see men "kill
time." Argument: On the battle-field, killing time when
the left and center are being routed! A fire brigade killing time when the city is in danger, and high up in the
lofty blazing blocks the shrieks of hundreds agonize for
deliverance! A life crew killing time when each moment
the roaring breakers threaten to swallow the sinking ship
with all on board! The engineer and fireman killing time
when the blazing cars are devouring the passengers pinioned down by broken timbers and heavy seats!

You killing time when the hosts of devils are captur-
ing and dragging down thousands! While the fires of
perdition blaze threateningly about the dwellings of lost
men! While the Judgment gathers blackness about the
old shattered hulks of time, and while the shrieks and
moans of the dying amid the blazing wrecks of despair are
ever in our ears! Yes, killing time! And the murderers
of the same will be held for trial at the coming judgment
day, and will be sentenced to death (eternal) for breach
of the commandment, "Thou shalt not kill."

Oh, your wasted moments spent in gossiping, evil-speaking, snoozing in bed, social chitchat, trifling and jesting, every moment heavily laden with eternal respon- sibilities. God and the devil, heaven and hell, time and eternity, sin and death, never take vacations. You who have but a narrow, allotted space to do up the work of preparation for a vast, boundless, unexplored eternity and who spend most of that handbreadth in vacations, Awake! Arouse! Arise! "No room for mirth or trifling here." No time for indulgence in any known sin.

> "Lo, on a narrow neck of land,
> 'Twixt two unbounded seas I stand,
> Secure, insensible,
> A point of time, a moment's space,
> Removes me to that heavenly place
> Or shuts me up in hell."

Time speeds away! The door will be shut! Time wasted. Life gone. Souls lost. Summer ended. Eternity here. Too late, too late!

OVERTURNERS

You have heard of the "overcomers," but did you ever hear of the "overturners"? They are the people of whom the Thessalonians said: "These that have turned the world upside down are come hither also" (Acts 17: 6). What a stir and commotion there is wherever they go. They find the world wrong side up, and they are "turning men (through God) from darkness to light and from the power of Satan unto God." "Thou art full of stirs, a tu- multuous city, a joyous city: thy slain men are not slain with the sword, nor dead in battle. For it is a day of trouble, and of treading down, and of perplexity of the Lord God of hosts in the valley of vision, breaking down the walls, and of crying to the mountains" (Isaiah 22: 2, 5).

Sinners in the church and out do not want to be disturbed and so they regard these overturners as "troublers in Israel." Those who find the most fault, as in the days of Paul, are backsliders in our own midst. We read in the context, "But the Jews which believed not took unto them certain lewd fellows of the baser sort and gathered a company, and set all the city in an uproar" (Acts 17:5). Indeed they saw the danger to their idols, their sins, their pleasures, if these men continued to succeed. Their complaint was, "These all do contrary to the decrees of Cæsar, saying there is another king, one Jesus" (Acts 17:7). Here is the testimony of an enemy.

No compromise with sin and wrong here for the sake of having influence with the sinner. Moses refused to be called the son of Pharaoh's daughter. If we would not be out and out in the matter, the worldling would stand it better. The only way to do is to go in and turn the works of the enemy clear over. "Ephraim is a cake not turned."

It must be turned over. Yet the carnal professor, Ephraim, would rather have the uncooked, sticky side turned up to catch the world, than to be turned toward God. Oh, what an outcry there is if you try to turn them over: "judging," "discouraging the people of God," "doing more harm than good," "bringing everybody to your notion," "righteous overmuch," and kindred speeches, while loving and clinging to their stickiness. But God's way is to turn them over, and the OVERTURNERS are always ready to do their part as coworkers with God. What an overturning there is when souls are seeking religion! How the old notions and ideas go overboard and how pliable and submissive they become to all the will of God. How quickly they say the cross is the way to glory. Oh, may God send out more overturners! They are multiplying and the songs and shouts of rejoicing foretell of the glad jubilee. Before, all their roots took fast hold of the world downward. Now, their tendencies are all upward. How they thirst and faint after God, and the eye of the soul is on Him

continually. No work is too hard if Jesus be there. Hallelujah! Join the overturners."

WHY?

A Free Methodist pastor asked me the other day the
question: "Why is it that our preachers were more successful in their earlier ministry than in after years?"
There may be special reasons in individual cases, but there
must be a general reason why this fact is true. To know
that it is true in many places we have only to look abroad
over the field and see that many who are exhorters, local
preachers, who in their first years of the conference rarely
ever had a barren year and saw, each year, numbers added
to the Lord, now go year after year without any special
breaking up under their labors. Why is this?

The tenor of the scripture shows the true gospel line
to be an increase of power and success. "And every branch
that beareth fruit He purgeth it, that it may bring forth
more fruit." The carnal heart suggests many excuses for
this unscriptural state of things, but God says, "They shall
bring forth fruit in old age." Outside of the few who are
"always abounding in the work of the Lord," and who, as
years advance, have increased the more in strength, the
young and inexperienced are the ones who bear the heat
of the day and hold the telling revivals, while many, who
were once successful, oppose, criticize, are more or less at
ease in Zion, and spend their energy and strength in laborious effort in another direction than for the salvation
of souls.

Some who oppose every new movement are so backslidden that if souls are not saved according to their notion, they will overthrow the work if in their power, even
if more souls are thus saved than they have brought to God
in many a year. The energetic brother who is all for God

they oppose with their broadside of compromise and death, if possible to bring him down to the same level of calm deathlikeness with themselves.

Others criticize. Thus they forfeit the little spiritual life left in them, by their unjust suspicions and unrighteous criticisms. These settle down on little, dying circuits with a few more-dead-than-alive members and preach little, visit less, practise self-denial least and complain bitterly because their little class does not better support them. Many, after a few years, deliberately decide between being soul-savers or preachers(?). Having decided to be preachers they slowly relax their efforts for soul saving and turn their attention to "firstly," "secondly," "thirdly." Now then you will see them studiously pouring over skeleton sermon books, and note-books in hand taking down the wise sayings of great preachers. They have fully set out on the tide to be preachers.

Perhaps before long they may be persuaded to take a course in a theological seminary. Thus they run on after a prize which they have set out to win. Instead of seeing many souls saved they now have the privilege of hearing their admirers say: "Was not that a grand sermon?" The die is now fully cast, and in proportion as they push in that direction, with that aim in view, in the same proportion they lose the power to prevail with God and man. To have consecrated their talents for soul-saving and preached with all their natural and acquired might with the sole aim of glorifying God, they would have earned its legitimate wages—the salvation of many souls. But they have left slowly but surely the glory of God out of the question and now they are barren indeed.

Here seems to be the key to the scene that is constantly transpiring before our eyes. Our schools, which are intended to subserve a proper end, are made tributary to this device of the devil, and so when a young man is called to preach there are many found who at once urge him to go to this or that seminary.

This is wrong. Keep the schools clean, and a place where the fire shall continually burn; then send the unsaved children there and the saved also whom God has not called. But when God calls, whether it be a fisherman at his net, a taxgatherer at his office, or a college graduate on a persecuting tour, let the nets, the office and the journey be forsaken at once and the God-called herald begin to lift up his voice everywhere. Then will he see his work rewarded with a hundred fold in this world and in the world to come everlasting life. We are following in the wake of the stranded churches around us, and will inevitably go on the same rocks, unless we call a halt.

AFFINITIES

This is the catchword for a most delusive and dangerous doctrine. Under its apparently harmless shadow is hidden a slimy and soul-damning system of spiritual wifery. The premises are that every soul has its perfect counterpart in the opposite sex, and if there is not congeniality in the marriage relation, if they do not feel the communion of kindred spirits, then they will find that other self outside of marriage bonds. There are two phases of this error. First, when it is plainly taught. Then in fact the marriage relation is only a form, while soul-union is sought elsewhere. Though outward rectitude is observed, the soul is wrapped in the slimy folds of spiritual adultery.

Wrong affections fire the heart. Inordinate affection classed, by God, with fornication (Col. 3:5), reigns in the soul. Any unlawful affection is an inordinate one. This is the seed of sin. It is but one step from the soul-embraces of inordinate affection to the sinful, sensual embraces of inordinate affection and then to the sinful, sensual embraces of actual sin. The one who, strong enough in himself to resist outward sin, teaches this foul doctrine does it to the utter undoing of weaker and more sensual souls. Its legitimate offspring are uncleanness and despair. "For this cause shall a man leave his father and mother and cleave unto his wife and they twain shall be one flesh."

The second phase is the delusive one where the inordinate affection comes disguised as a proper affection. Many souls that would turn away disgusted if the open doctrine was taught are snared by this "angel of light." Some one has been a great help to another, the instrument of conversion or great good. The enemy comes saying this is your father, your mother, your son, your daughter in Jesus. You think you have only love for them as a Christian. The deception is complete. The unwary soul is snared. The same inordinate affection is doing its deadly work, and unless there is an awakening the terrible fall is sure. May God protect His little ones from these snares. The only safety is to keep so lost in God that no flesh spot can touch the soul.

An interest in another that draws one toward him, and leaves one disturbed and restless in his absence, is of the enemy. Avoid it. If either phase of these affections has taken possession of your soul and been yielded to, do not profess holiness. That vile affection has polluted your soul and left its slimy traces along the entire length of your affections. It must die. It emanates alone from the foul life of carnality. It smells of brimstone and leaves the plague spots of hell in its track.

Confession to God of our carnal state is needed, deep and pungent. This affection inordinate, springing out of the putrid depths of the carnal mind, must be severed from the soul. Oh, what a deliverance! The affections which the will could not control are brought into line with

purity. God takes up the entire being. Satan comes and
finds nothing in us. Our affections are set on things
above and not on things on the earth. May we all be
sanctified wholly and preserved blameless unto the coming
of our Lord Jesus Christ. Amen.

WORK

What can be more extraordinary than the Bible language applied to work? "Work, for the night cometh, when
no man can work." "Always abounding in the work of the
Lord." "Whatsoever thy hand findeth to do, do it with thy
might." "The violent take it by force." "Run, with patience, the race." These are expressions covering the ut-
most of effort for God. No lost time is involved. Every
moment employed. No languid movement. "Do it with
thy might." Yet on every side, if any one gets in earnest,
comes the cry, "Take it easier; you are killing your workers." Think of a man taking it easy on the edge of Ve-
suvius! No room for trifling or ease here in this smoulder-
ing crater of time!

At the time of the Chatsworth horror, while shrieks
and cries rent the air, and the victims, pinned down under
the broken car timbers, saw the flames surely approaching
them, and while men, with the energy of despair, dug up
the clods and dirt with their hands to put out the fire,
some ladies found a man, a little removed from the accident, lying on a Pullman mattress. They asked him where
he was wounded. He said, "Nowhere." They said, "Then
give us this mattress for the wounded." He said, "No, I
have paid for it and propose to keep it." They said, "You
will not," and secured help and dragged the heartless
wretch from his place of ease.

But what is this compared to those who take their
ease while the flames of hell kindle on the poor victims of

sin, pinioned under the wrecks of time. Preachers who work as though there was no judgment to come; professors who walk and talk as though there was no "lake of fire." How many does drink destroy every year? How many thousands do evil habits and pride bring down to the grave? What is the number of the host sacrificed to the Moloch of lust and wrong eating? Can you marshall these unnumbered multitudes? Then shall there be a hue and cry if one man or woman shall literally "wear out" for the Master? "He that loveth his life shall lose it, and he that loseth his life, for my sake, shall preserve it unto life eternal." Not recklessly nor presumptuously, but in earnest. agonizing work for the lost, until the weary wheels stand still, "the golden bowl be broken," and the Master says, "It is enough."

Oh, for men and women who will prove what they so often sing, "Let me die at my post." Oh, for a thousand self-sacrificing ones, who "love not their lives unto the death," and are ready for sacrifice or service in any land; who are as ready, like Napoleon's soldiers, to make a bridge of their bodies to carry others over, as to sing the conqueror's song. Amen! Amen!

DEAD TO THE WORLD

Very often when souls are seeking the distinct blessing of holiness, you hear those who are instructing them telling them to "die out to the world." Also, while preaching, some teach that in order for the soul to be cleansed they must "die to the world." This teaching is confusing and delusive. "Whosoever is born of God overcometh the world," saith the apostle John. This Scripture teaches that the justified soul has overcome, or is dead to the world. Must not justified souls have victory over their friends, over earthly riches, over worldly pleasures, over sinful appetites? Yes, we say. Very well then, why confuse the seeking soul by teaching that they must die to the world when seeking holiness? A justification that does not deliver from the world is worth nothing. Let us keep the line clear and evident between us and the world. There is a death for the soul seeking entire holiness. Not to ,the world but to the "old man." This death we must taste. It is a real death. The "old man" will continually try to turn our attention to something else in order to shield himself. Rev. F. D. Brooke once illustrated this point well. He said when they were boys on the farm they had a dog they used to play with, and the dog would catch and pull them to the ground. One day his brother set the dog on him and as he saw he could not get away, he pointed ahead and began to call, "Seek, seek." The dog thinking there was something ahead ran on and left him. So when the soul is stirred by the evil within and begins to seek for purity, the "old man" begins to cry, "Seek, seek," and tries to turn the attention of the soul to something else. Let us hold steadily to God's living truth. Justification delivers from the world, entire holiness delivers from the carnal mind.

MANIFESTATIONS

A clear understanding of the mind of the Lord with reference to manifestations is necessary to a good experience. There are two dangers that everybody is exposed to in a greater or less degree.

First, quenching the Spirit and failing to obey God.

Second, giving manifestations greater weight than God does, and thinking that they alone are evidences of a good experience. Either mistake is fatal. That God gives His saints various exercises when under the Spirit, He declares. "And there are diversities of operations, but it is the same God which worketh all in all" (1 Cor. 12:6).

Some men lay down their human rules as to what the operations of the Spirit are, but God says, "Diversities." There are circumstances in which God's saints leap for joy. Many (even some professing holiness) are opposed to jumping. But Jesus says, "Blessed are ye when men shall hate you, and when they shall separate you from their company, and reproach you, and cast out your name as evil for the Son of man's sake. Rejoice ye in that day and leap for joy" (Luke 26:22, 23). This is no figure of speech. It is a plain declaration and those who have gone through the experience, especially when it came from friends and false brethren, have felt that superabundant joy. Some oppose any noise which is not an intelligent shout. The prophet Isaiah says, "Cry out and shout, thou inhabitant of Zion: for great is the Holy One of Israel in the midst of thee" (Isaiah 12:6). The prophet Zechariah says, "They shall drink, and make a noise as through wine" (Zech. 9:15). This text refers to the saints of God, and is an exact prophecy, fulfilled to the letter at Pentecost. when the opposers cried out. "These men are full of new wine" (Acts 2:13).

The saints, when full of the Spirit, are variously exercised. The Bible sanctions, by example and precept, falling under the power of God, leaping for joy, shouting, crying, and laughing with holy joy. These exercises, when the individual is led to them by the Spirit, should not be quenched. If men oppose, or preachers cry down, let the Holy Ghost have His own way. According to the Word of God, all who are filled with the Spirit will manifest it in some manner.

The second danger comes in judging experience by manifestations. When one judges the holiness of another by manifestations, he is wide of the mark. This is no criterion, except when accompanied by a holy heart and life. The great danger of self comes in when we begin to seek exercises instead of God, or when we seek the manner

of exercises instead of leaving God to lead us as He will.
Let us remember that we may be unsaved and go through
all these exercises; that they are no criterion of experience; that we should not seek them, nor desire any special
manifestation. If we guard these points and unrestrained-
ly give ourselves up to God, seeking only more of God, we
will have "indeed freedom," "run and not be weary,"
"have our mouth filled with laughter and our tongue with
singing," and sometimes be unable to tell "whether in the
body or out of the body."

HOLINESS

What is it and how obtained? "Holiness is wholeness."
It is a state of being, through the agency of the atonement,
that brings us back to the purity held by the human race
before the fall. When a soul is wholly sanctified it is as
pure as angels and relatively as pure as God. "Be ye
therefore perfect, even as your Father in heaven is perfect."
This does not mean absolute perfection, but relative or con-
ditional purity or perfection. They may become impure.
They are not perfect in judgment, but in purpose. Not
perfect in knowledge, but in obedience.

To obtain holiness there is necessary: First, light;
second, conviction; third, confession; fourth, crucifixion;
fifth, saving or appropriating faith. Faith, in general
terms, stands out as the sole condition of entire holiness;
for without faith not one step can the seeker take toward
God. He must have faith with the enlightening, faith
with the conviction, and faith with the confession. But
appropriating faith is based upon conditions that are as
inviolate as the faith itself.

The common method of teaching that holiness is obtained by consecration and faith, is very blinding and can
be proven from Scripture only by giving the words a

strained meaning, such as they are not capable of bearing. First, light. No soul will seek God until he has light upon his heart. The Word of God is a lamp unto our feet, and a light unto our path, and through the Word we get light. The Spirit shines upon the Word and reveals the truth to us. God uses His people also. "Mark the perfect man, and behold the upright, for the end of that man is peace." "Living epistles, known and read of all men." To this end, reading of the Word, preaching, expounding, teaching, and testimony in the Spirit, are a necessity. By these means the light shines. The state of the soul is revealed to the understanding. "The depths of pride, self-will and hell appear."

The old man which is "corrupt according to the deceitful lusts" is discovered in his hiding place. The carnal mind which "is enmity against God" is shown in his opposings. The body of sin, the seed of sin, containing the germ of every carnal manifestation, the vital chit of every foul fruit of the flesh, becomes manifest under the blazing light of God in all its native ugliness.

The light does not show one up as being not very bad and the old nature trained almost to purity's perfection, and some one else as the one whose thoughts and the imagination of whose heart is evil and that continually. But the light discovers to every one that "from the sole of the foot even unto the head there is no soundness in it; but wounds, and bruises, and putrifying sores: they have not been closed, neither mollified with ointment."

This brings the soul to conviction. Not a light, surface feeling that is easily dispelled by a sociable neighbor, or a good dinner; but a deep, increasing, unendurable agony of soul, that cries out, "O wretched man that I am! who shall deliver me from the body of this death?"

Conviction settles down upon the soul. The image of the enemy of all righteousness is seen in the carnal mind, the mark of the beast; the same leprosy that shall forever drive the soul from the companionship of the holy. Then does the soul loathe, abhor, and turn away from all earthly sights and sounds. With Paul, while darkness gathers round, so far as earthly ambitions are concerned, if necessary without food and drink for three days he cries to God. No pleasure to the man who feels the weight of sin's death within him. Not that length of time or outward expressions are an essentiality here, but that the knowledge of the depraved state revealed to a justified soul will produce the most intense conviction with its necessary accompaniments.

The next step is confession. The soul addresses itself to God, against a common enemy, and acknowledges the state within. If we confess our unrighteousness He is "faithful and just to cleanse us from all unrighteousness." Not of necessity must the confession be made to man, except when men have been involved through the deception of the carnal mind, but to God. Not of past deeds or sin, but of the hidden qualities, propensities, and manifestations of the man of sin within. When the conviction is deep and pungent the confession will not be forced, but will come forth as a relief to the anguish-stricken soul. This process of the Spirit, confession, will bring the soul to the human part of the crucifixion.

The light and the confession bring to view the man of sin. Instance, when the soul is wrapped in the strong coils of covetousness and avarice, confession brings to light more fully the nature within and delivers over the "old man" to the Holy Ghost, who doeth the work. *We can not kill self, only in the sense that we can confess the carnal mind; hand it over, renounce it, and will its death.* This the Scripture means when it says, "They that are Christ's have crucified the flesh, with the affections and lusts." Have crucified. We need not fear a Bible expression. Given in a Bible sense, consecration does not cover the foregoing. To attempt to make it, is to strain it beyond its legitimate meaning. You cannot consecrate the carnal mind; hence if it can not be consecrated, it remains there, necessitating another condition to the faith that sanctifies, which we have called crucifixion.

The soul has now arrived at the place where faith appropriates the blessing. In the majority of cases, we doubt not, faith will be simultaneous with this point of contact. There need be no long and labored effort to get the soul to believe, for when he has had the light, felt the depths of nature, confessed to God, crucified the "old man," and without reservation or equivocation, handed over his powers to God's service and glory, it is easy to have faith in God. The necessary accompaniments of holiness are assurance, purity, peace and power. Following the appropriating faith, the witness of the Spirit brings to the soul the assurance of the work completed.

The soul is pure, the movements of sin are gone. No motions of fleshly lusts that war against the soul. No inward stirrings. The wisdom that is from above is first pure, then peaceable. The peace of God succeeds the whirlwind of battle that has agitated the soul. "Great peace have they that love thy law, and nothing shall offend them." They have constant peace.

Power is a necessary accompaniment of holiness. A powerless soul is an unholy soul. Carnality is weakness. When souls are seeking power they should be seeking purity. The Pentecostal enduement of power was purity of heart. Mark Peter's words, "And put no difference between us and them, purifying our hearts by faith." "But tarry ye in the city of Jerusalem, until ye be endued with power from on high." True holiness knows the nature from which it was delivered, the soul-honesty that was necessary to the work, and the Holy Spirit, who, as active agent, accomplished the work and brought in the great deliverance and the freedom from warring elements, the music of peace that flows through the soul, the power

divine which upholds, fills and makes it mighty for battle
and for conquest unto the glorious end.

TITHES AND OFFERINGS

How many to-day are robbing God! God's demand
upon every Christian is one-tenth of the increase. The system of tithing does not belong to the Jewish system of religion alone. The patriarchs tithed in the days of Abra-
ham, for after the recapture of the king of Sodom, Abra-
ham gave tithes of the spoil of Melchisedec, king of Salem,
which Melchisedec was a type of Christ.

The Son of man, when reproving the scribes and
Pharisees, said, "Ye pay tithe of mint and anise and cum-
min, and have omitted the weightier matters of the law,
judgment, mercy, and faith: these ought ye to have done,
and not to leave the other undone" (Matt. 23 : 23).

The Son of God endorsed this truth thus plainly.
How many then are robbing Jesus Christ. They do not
give Him His tenth. That is His rent that He charges
for His air, sunshine, earth and rain. We, however, have
the pleasure of paying it out according to His will. If
this were practised everywhere, we have no circuit so poor
but a preacher would be well supplied. Ten families
would support a preacher, and ten preachers would send
a missionary and support him on the field.

This is only God's right. He complains bitterly and
says, "Ye have robbed me, even this whole nation." It is
only common honesty. The neglect of it stunts our souls,
injures our joy, and paralyzes the work of the Lord. If
the people of God only gave Him what is righteously His,
the banner of the cross would soon wave in every land.
God's money is laid up for a "rainy day," or, worse if possible, to be willed to unsaved children and relatives, that
they may use it to fight God with, and strengthen themselves in their strongholds of covetousness and pride.

Will you rob God? Beware! He will have His own. If you do not give it to Him, He will take it out of you in calamities that shall overtake you. But those who tithe think they have done all that is necessary. They have done nothing. They have only given God back that which belongs to Him. If you want to give to God, then you must make Him an offering. God does not want to be robbed in offerings. He asks His people, over and above the tenth, to make offerings from their nine-tenths. Thus will they glorify God.

The one who preaches this truth is called grasping, and few dare to do their whole duty for fear of man. But the truth must be proclaimed, and if the one who proclaims it is counted an evil-doer let him glorify God on this behalf. "Bring ye all the tithes into the storehouse, that there may be meat in mine house, and prove me now herewith, saith the Lord of hosts, if I will not open you the windows of heaven, and pour you out a blessing, that there shall not be room enough to receive it" (Mal. 3: 10).

THE DRY BONE VALLEY CIRCUIT

Never perhaps was a preacher called to travel upon a more discouraging circuit than was Ezekiel. But the first point that we notice is that he was carried there by the Spirit. This of itself is enough to give courage to a true child of God. None can hope to succeed when ambition, selfishness or desire for ease has dictated his labor. But when the Spirit not only leads, but carries the man over all obstacles and opposition, he can be courageous on the Dry Bone Valley Circuit. We do not hear Ezekiel saying: "Well, this is the hardest circuit in the conference, and I know there must have been wire-pulling or I would have gone to a better field. I will pack up and leave." No, God had sent him and he began to look for divine orders. The first was to look his field over thoroughly. This he did and he found "many bones, and behold they were very dry."

God does not send His servants to work in the dark. He wants them to know the circumstances and then like a skilful surgeon take the proper steps to remedy the trouble. God did not hide the state of the circuit from Ezekiel. He showed him many bones and they were very dry. There was not even an old saint to say, Amen! There was not one that was gasping to keep alive. They were all dry bones, and very dry at that. But we hear no murmurings, no discouraged words. God says, "Can these bones live?" Ezekiel casts the burden back on the Lord and says, "Lord, thou knowest." That is the same as though he had said, "There is no help in the human, but thou, O Lord, canst do all things; whatever thou commandest me to do, I am here to do."

Then God commanded him to preach to the dry bones. Without a word he began to say, "O dry bones, hear the word of the Lord!" Oh, what faith in God is here exemplified. The preacher had not preached long until there came a shaking among the dry bones. "Bone came to his bone." Many want a revival, but they are not ready for it on the shaking line. How many societies need this shaking. It will bring bone to his bone. Old troubles will be gotten out of the way and there will be a coming together, a confessing, a repenting and making right that will prepare the way of God's great work of grace.

The shaking may not be a very pleasant process, but it is a very profitable one. There may be noises and motions that may not seem very respectable or cultured, but if bone comes to bone and the flesh covers them, never mind. In a valley full of dry bones there may be a violent demonstration to break loose from the mass and find the normal place, but let the Spirit lead and keep hands off, and God will see to the results.

By this time there was much encouragement on the Dry Bone Valley Circuit. The next command to prophesy to the winds to breathe on the slain was quickly obeyed and lo! where there had been a valley very full of dry bones, "stood up an exceeding great army." Now the faith was lost in sight and the troubles of the past were forgotten in the victories of the present. Agreeable surroundings were not an evidence of being in divine order.

Never was Ezekiel more in divine order than when he set out to travel the Dry Bone Valley Circuit. No official board to stand by; not one old mother in Israel to clap her hands and say, "Amen!" Nothing but death. But God brought one live man there, and the Dry Bone Valley Circuit had to change its name to the Resurrection Valley Circuit. God makes us alive to bring us in contact with death, for His glory.

WALK IN THE LIGHT

The Apostle John makes walking in the light the condition of sanctification. The meaning of the apostle is generally given rather vaguely. But there is no need of indefiniteness. The Bible definition of light is: "Whatsoever doth make manifest is light." The light of God upon the heart of a sinner shows him his sins, the remedy for sin, and the end of a life of sin. The light upon the heart of a believer shows him the carnal nature hidden deep within. Here is the necessity of walking in the light. God lets the light shine upon the carnality of the heart, and if we walk in that light, it discloses to us our state of soul more and more. If we love the light we will hasten to walk in it. The saved soul does love the light, but so deceitful is the carnal mind that it is hard to call the self-life, which is so threaded through our being, carnality. Mr. Wesley saw it when he sang, "Chase this self-love

through all my heart, through all its latent mazes thou."
To walk in the light is to acknowledge the carnal mind.
Then as we see its manifestations, to confess them. The
great trouble of getting souls to confess their carnal nature is the cause of much shallowness of experience.

Men who are naturally very prudent and saving hate
much to confess their covetousness; others hate to confess
their pride. Many are like the Brahmin who had a microscope given to him. In examining his rice he found mi-
crobes in it. He knew they were meat, and his religion
said he must not eat meat. He could not get along without his rice, so he made up his mind the cheapest way was
to throw his microscope away.

Just so, many draw back from the light of God when
it shines so clearly upon their heart-sin and shows them
that what they have so long petted and thought so fondly
was a very satisfactory part of their proper being is, in
fact, nothing less than the carnal mind, the fell destroyer
of mankind. Then comes the struggle, and often the soul
throws away the light and wanders in the darkness of a
superficial experience. Whenever the light shines upon
any manifestation of the carnal nature, we may then
know that the body of sin is there.

Here again many sad mistakes are made. When the
light shines, instead of walking steadily in it, they get a
victory over that manifestation, repress the "old man" and
leave him in the depths below. God's light will not fail
to show us our state. Then open your eyes while it shines
upon the foe within. How we will be astonished! How
the light will reveal the slimy, putrid monster within.
"Corrupt." What depths of meaning. All veiled in darkness. We know it not because we do not walk in the light.
The light shines but we do not advance in the light.
"Awake thou that sleepest, and arise from the dead and
Christ shall give thee light."

Now walk in the light. As you confess, your heart

will break up and you will feel your great Deliverer near.
Walking in the light will bring us to the point of VIC-
TORY. We need only to walk in the light and we shall
know just what the will of the Lord is. Light makes
everything plain, shines away all doubt, and gives us to
see the track of life which leads direct to the mount of
crucifixion and the hour of deliverance.

"WITHOUT THE CAMP"

The apostle used this figure to typify a necessary condition of salvation. There is nothing popular about the
religion of Jesus. The man who took the scapegoat outside the camp, took the reproach of the people with him,
and was himself involved for the time being in the reproach. Thus Jesus suffered outside the gate. He bore
the reproach. He did not die in the city surrounded by
friends. We are exhorted to go forth unto Him without
the camp. "If we suffer with Him, we shall also reign
with Him." Many who want the glory are not ready to
take the "lone way." But the real saints of God are ready
to follow wherever they can see the footsteps of their
Master. It means to stand alone.

We can not be saved by companies. We must learn
to stand alone. It is pleasant to have good companionship, but the child of God is ready to stand alone in the
breach. Some are good soldiers in a crowd; but how few
can follow Jesus alone when all the reproach falls on their
devoted heads. It means to receive the reproach of the
multitudes. Some think that because the multitudes reproach you, you must be wrong. Jesus received the reproach of the throng; so must those who go with Him. It
will come seemingly like an overflowing tide, and the weak
and faint-hearted will fall in with it. But the resolute
few will boldly withstand it for Jesus' sake.

The call of God is for those who will go outside the camp. There are plenty of camp loungers, plenty who love to eat the good things and enjoy the ease, but God wants those who will take reproach and hardship outside the camp. Let not God's little ones fear. Only be sure that you follow the Master, that your lives tell for Him, and you will find Him also outside the camp. Let not the one who loves popularity think to find it in the way of the Nazarene. He will find the joy that the world knows not of, he will find the way of life, but the applause of the world goes in another line. This is the line where comes the glory. The saints of God find it better to take it and the glory that follows, than to have an empty profession without God in the soul.

It is a place of freedom outside the camp. No straight jacket nor ecclesiastical red tape to kill out the life of the soul but a blessed freedom in the Lord. Amen! Then away to the field, the battle, the reproach. Fight for your Master, die for Him, and enter into your reward.

A PESTILENT FELLOW

This was the name given to the Apostle Paul by his accusers. He made a stir wherever he went and did not allow men to sleep the sleep of death. He shook the very foundations of sin and a backslidden Judaism by the thunders of his God-given truth. The men, thus disturbed, sought means to rid themselves of this troubler, so they began to call him a "pestilent fellow."

When a man takes a stand by the old paths and cries out against compromise, and denounces compromise in dress and church buildings; when he stirs up sleepy preachers, "dumb dogs that can not bark," it is very convenient to begin to cry out "a pestilent fellow." But God's little ones know the joyful ring. They understand where the ark of God is and they will be ready to take their stand by the truth of God.

This cry against Paul drove him out of Judea and sent him a prisoner to a distant land. But it only enlarged his circuit and gave him a chance of preaching the gospel from the throne of the Cæsars. Here at Rome was the gathering place of the world, and as the apostle preached, his words were carried to all parts of the world. These cries against the true children of God may sway the people for the time being, but God has His hand over His own work and will never suffer it to be tested only so that the pure gold shall shine forth undimmed. Let all of God's little ones keep humble; let them not return any of the rallying cries of Satan but keep to the work of God and surely God will make the wrath of man to praise Him.

CHAPTER X

POEMS

TO MY WIFE
BIRTHDAY VERSES

What, are you twenty-six years old?
  Half of your years, perhaps, are told;
Eternity comes on apace
  And time is distant in the race.

Put in the remnant of your days
  So each one shall be good for praise,
And naught in one to mar your joy,
  But swell your bliss without alloy.

Your length of time? It matters none,
  So but your Father's will be done;
May each succeeding birthday find
  You all for God in heart and mind.

November 22, 1886.   HUSBAND

BIRTHDAY PRESENT TO MY WIFE

WRITTEN ON NOVEMBER 22, 1891, IDA'S THIRTY-FIRST BIRTHDAY.

Gladsome day returning
  Marks another year,
With its joys and mourning,
  With its hopes and fear:
Marks another layer
  On the wall of life
(Through our Great Preserver)
  For my precious wife.

Stormy, cold November,
  Twenty-second day,
Day I shall remember,
  Oft in tuneful lay;

Out of it came beauty,
  Sparkling forth with life,
Music, worth and duty—
  Ida May, my wife.

Fourteen years together
  Have we walked as one,
In all sorts of weather,
  Night and noonday sun;
But the latest birthday
  Finds our hearts more true
Than when in our heyday
  Journeying was new.

Little Ruth and Carrie,
  These the precious gems—
And our eldest Mary—
  In our diadem,
May this day forever,
  Mark its moments trod,
Faltering, no, never,
  Nearer all to God.

Much have you to live for,
  Great the work to do;
All the strength you pray for
Shall be given to you.
Life is not a trifle,
  Living do your best,
Do not one power stifle—
  Heaven will bring you rest.

ALL FAIR

Fair thou art, my love,
  Glorious within,
Sweeter than a lovely song,
Purified from sin.

Warble out thy soul
  To thy glorious King,
He whose balm hath made thee whole:
  Let His praises ring.

Let thy ransomed powers
All to Him be given;
Fill thy work days' glorious hours,
Then He'll give thee *Heaven*.

He called me to him one day just before he left for Africa
and said, "I want to leave you a check that will be sufficient for
all your needs while I am away."   My check was Matthew 6:26:
"Behold the fowls of the air, for they sow not, neither do they
reap, nor gather into barns; yet your heavenly Father feedeth
them. Are ye not much better than they?"   He also gave me the
little poem recorded below, which he wrote for my comfort.

I. M. D.

HEDGED IN

The saints of God are safe
From all assaults of hell,
For Satan hath himself declared
That saints in safety dwell,

For God hath hedged us in,
And Satan powerless stands;
His rage and hate and hellish spite
Our Father countermands.

No robbers, storms or death
Can cause a saint to fear;
They rage without that God-made hedge,
And Father's always near.

CHORUS

Hath He not made a hedge
On every side around
About thy house and all thou hast,
And caused thee to abound?

WORKERS' WARNING

Precious worker, danger signals
Float around thee; take thou **heed**;
Bide thee in thy place till Jesus
To another field field shall lead.

Siren voices most enticing
  Would allure thee from thy trust;
Honeyed words, mere Sodom's apples,
  'Neath the pressure turn to dust.

Friends will urge, constrain, persuade you,
  Point a better, easier way;
Anything beside, the tempter
  Will suggest. Oh, haste away!
Seek another field of labor,
  Leave your burdens and your band,
And in other fields you'll surely
  More respect and love command.

Precious jewels thou hast gathered
  For thy crowning by and by,
When thy Lord shall call His faithful
  To their welcome in the sky.
Wilt thou run the risk of losing
  All thy trophies, all thy gain?
Trifle with the souls thy Savior
  Purchased with His blood and pain?

Thou hast felt 'twas God that called thee.
  Hast thy God released thee? Hark!
To turn from His will and pleasure
  Is to wander in the dark.
Bide you in your place, dear worker,
  Till your Lord shall bring release,
Then by death or Spirit's whisper
  It will come on wings of peace.

ALL FOR PRECIOUS SOULS

Earthly friendships all are riven,
  All for precious souls;
Hopes, ambitions, joys are given,
  All for precious souls.

Precious Jesus, all in all,
  Conquered at Thy feet I fall,
Longing for Thy faintest call—
  All for precious souls.

Home, sweet home, no longer mine,
　All for precious souls;
Murmur not my soul, nor pine,
　All for precious souls.

Earth's fair scenes allure me not,
　All thy pleasures I've forgot,
Turn I from thy fairest spot—
　All for precious souls.

Welcome now, reproach and scorn,
　All for precious souls;
Joyful tread the paths of thorn,
　All for precious souls.

Dearest friend may pass me by.
　Taunts and threats my courage try,
Welcome all as swift I fly—
　All for precious souls.

Suffer on, my soul, till death,
　All for precious souls;
Pleading with my latest breath,
　All for precious souls.

Earth recedes, thy work is done,
Toil is past, triumph begun;
Brighter shine than noonday sun
　With thy precious souls.

FOR THE WORKERS

I've no room in my soul but for Jesus,
　No time but to serve Him each day;
I've no word but to speak out His praises,
　No joy but His presence alway.

I've no crosses to bear but are helpful,
　Nor sorrows but bring greater joy;
I've no trials but make me shine brighter,
　No tests but my hope can destroy.

I've no fears but are vanished forever,
　No sins but are under the blood,
No foes but I've freely forgiven;
　I am clean, washed in Calvary's flood.

I've no earth house, but one sure in heaven,
  And there I'll forever abide;
My Jesus invites, and I'm going
  To sing evermore by His side.

CONSECRATION

I consecrate my life to Thee, dear Lord,
To labor with my might, call nothing hard,
Use all my strength with every passing day,
Then ask for more, and hasten on my way;
Pluck brands from out the burning while I live.
Then heavenward fall, and falling, heaven receive.

I consecrate my time, my length of days.
And every moment shall speak forth Thy praise.
E'en to old age will I renew my strength,
Mount up on wings as eagles, and, at length.
When all my time is spent in Thine employ,
Drop off this flesh and enter into joy.

I consecrate my money, Lord; 'tis Thine.
And not a mite will I speak of as mine.
Naught will I spend in selfishness or ease,
But seek alone, Thee only, Lord, to please.
Strive not to lay up treasure here below,
But all my treasure safe in heaven bestow.

I consecrate my powers of soul and mind,
In Thee my powers shall meet employment find,
My judgment and my will and memory store.
Imaginations, thoughts, shall evermore
Be captive to my Christ, the crucified;
Each all their work perform, yet in Thee hide,
Affection's wealth, pour incense on Thy head,
And grosser appetites forever dead.

I consecrate my body, yes, I may
Serve Thee with e'en this mortal lump of clay.
My eyes, my ears, my tongue, my feet, my hands,
Shall quiet be, or haste at Thy commands.
And for Thy glory they shall be kept meet,
Yea e'en the food, which by Thy grace I eat.
My transient home, the raiment which I wear.—
In this and all. Thy glory my sole care.

I consecrate my home, my friends, my all,
And forth I go, heeding Thy gracious call.
Ready for any place, afar or near;
The place that others shun I will not fear,
But gladly go, if I may only bring
One wanderer more to serve my God and King.

I consecrate to suffer naught within
That presence shows of dark orig'nal sin.
But by God's grace drive deep the 'venging spike,
That to the carnal heart-life death shall strike;
Suffer no signs of wrath, impatience, pride,
Of hellish lust, or malice prone to hide
Deeply within, or fear, or love of praise,
But, by Thy blood made pure, outlive my days.

I consecrate to do, to dare,
To suffer with my Savior, and to bear
Hardness, as soldiers should, on every field,
To run the race, to weakness never yield.
Refuse all honor, ease, or earthly store,
Take up the cross, deny self more and more,
Bend all my energies to save the lost
AND WITH SOME STARS, GAIN HEAVEN
    AT ANY COST.

TRACK OF TRIBULATION

There's a track of tribulation
  By the saints of ages trod,
'Tis the highway of the ransomed,
  And it leadeth up to God.
'Tis the way the Man of Sorrows
  Journeyed in His low estate,
When He sought the lost and found them—
  Was there ever love so great?

Lost, yea, lost with none to rescue,
  Arms too short, and strength too small,
Till the Son of God came swiftly
  With a love that conquered all.
Came to poverty and scorning,
  Came to mocking and distress,
Came to final joy and triumph
  Over sin and hell and death.

Oh, the scene that spread before Him
  In this lost and ruined world,
Where the hosts of hell are gathered,
  And rebellion's flag's unfurled.
Like the mighty rushing torrent,
  Swift to hell the millions sped,
Sinking down, forever sinking,
  In the region of the dead.

Scenes of Nazareth and Gethsemane,
  Pilate's hall and Herod's throne,
Scenes where all with one consenting
  Did their blessed Lord disown.
Was there ever love so gracious?
  On this tribulation track,
Patiently He journeyed onward,
  Nor did give one answer back.

Lonely watch of dark Gethsemane,
  Prone upon the cold, damp ground,
Burdened with the sins of many,
  With no friends to gather round,
Forced the blood from all its channels,
  Trickling down from every pore,
Witness dire of pain and anguish
  Which for thee the Savior bore.

Tumult fills the hall of judgment,
  Silent stands the patient One.
Crown of thorns, spittings, revilings,
  Shower upon God's only Son.
"Upon us and our children,
  Be His blood," they fiercely cry.
Crucify Him, crucify Him!
  On to Calvary! He must die!

Up the track of tribulation
  Patiently the Lord doth go,
Bearing on His back the burden,
  End of all His pain and woe.
Blessed cross! which Jesus carried
  Mid that dark tumultuous throng,
Clasp I to my heart forever—
  This the theme of all my song.

Crowning scene of love at Calvary,
  Rugged cross and cruel nails,
E'en the thief who suffered with Him
  Bitterly his Lord assails.
Gushing blood—a fountain flowing
  From His feet, His hands, His side,
Moves no stony heart to pity;
  They His tears and love deride.

Nature draws her veil of pity
  O'er the sufferings of the Lord,
Darkness dense, and then the earthquake,
  Sympathy for Nature's God.
Oh, the love immense, unfathomed,
  Even at His latest breath
Beams His eyes with love and pity,
  And with love He conquered death.

Look ye here! ye scorned followers
  Of your persecuted Lord.
Gaze upon those dying features,
  Listen to the wondrous words,
Even now in keenest anguish
  Greater far than mortal knew:
Father, be merciful, forgive them,
  For they know not what they do.

Thus the saints of all the ages
  Took the track their Savior trod,
Glorying in the roughest pathways,
  Leading only to their God.
Tribulation worketh patience,
  Tribulation's hottest fire
Brings the tribulation glory,
  Mid its flames they mount the higher.

They were stoned, were sawn asunder,
  Tortured, tempted, mocked and scourged;
To the deserts and the mountains,
  To the dens and caves were urged;
Walked on thorns of persecution,
  Drank the bitterest cups of gall,
Mixed with tribulation glory,
  Shining conqueror over all.

See the footprints of our Savior
  O'er His royal track divine;
And apostles, fathers, martyrs,
  All have walked this heavenly line.
Hail, all hail, reproach and sorrow,
  Partners of Christ's sufferings here,
Partners of His final triumph,
  Through the grand eternal years.

Know ye not this track of trial
  Is the only way to heaven?
They shall suffer persecution,
  Who to Christ their all have given.
But the waves shall not o'erflow thee,
  And the flames shall do no harm;
He that to the end endureth
  Safe shall be from all alarm.

Who are these and whither came they?
  These that stand before the throne
Clothed in robes of spotless whiteness,
  Known to saints, to angels known?
These are they who washed their garments
  In the Savior's precious blood;
And through tribulation's fires,
  Now they stand before their God.

                    —Written in 1886.

ALL THINGS

Romans 2: 36

For of Him are all things,
  The Lord of the sky;
He rides on a cherub,
  He ruleth on high;
By Him were created
  All things that exist,
And by Him they now
  And shall ever consist.

CHORUS

Let the morning stars sing,
Let the loud anthems ring,

Let all that hath breath catch the word;
Let the worlds join the song.
Let creation's vast throng
Swell the anthems of praise to the Lord.

And through Him are all things,
He holds in His hand
The worlds He's created,
And by Him they stand.
The least grain of sand
Or the mightiest sphere
In His smile remain,
In His wrath disappear.

And to Him are all things,
His glory they sing,
Both now and forever,
Their Almighty King;
While all things created
A loud chorus raise,
And the universe echoes
The notes of His praise.

The following to Mrs. H. A. Coon, who prayed for Mr. Dake
while seeking the experience of holiness.

BIRTHDAY TOKEN

Dear auntie, receive this small token,
A breath from the heart of your child,
Remembrance of love never broken,
But joined in a God reconciled.
Long years have you traveled life's pathway.
In comparison mine are but few,
But the sunshine of your closing life's day.
Does my spirit and body renew.

So this is the fifty-ninth chorus
In your sweet, joyful pilgrimage song.
And loved ones—to Him who hath borne us
Through trials—the chorus prolong;
Each year counts a verse in the hymning
Of praise to our Savior divine,
And the birthday brings in the glad summing,
The chorus in which we all join.

Deep, deep rolls the bass of thy sorrow,
  And pain's piercing tenor runs high,
Then notes changing with coming to-morrow.
  All hail! for it's coming draws nigh.
The alto of love—a hosanna,
With notes purest, sweetest, though strong,
And the Spirit's full glorious soprano
  Hath blended the whole into song.

The sharps and flats—discord dire,
  If standing alone, out of place,
They add to the harmony, fire
  As trials to souls bringeth grace,
The rests often seem to be wanting,
  For the song is sung "while 'tis day,"
But for thee rest eternal is waiting,
  Where working is resting for aye.

O'er each verse crescendo appeareth,
  An increase of peace and of power,
And diminuendo applieth
  To the world with its swift passing hour.
The key is the key of Salvation,
  The tune, is the Holy Ghost joy.
And the strain, "in this world tribulation,"
  Bringeth sweetness that naught can destroy.

The swan that before never singeth,
  At death sings a song passing sweet,
And the curfew at eventide ringeth,
  When sunbeams from darkness retreat.
So thy song gathers sweetness from sorrow,
  And lightens despair's darkest night.
The last verse thou'lt sing on the morrow,
  All heaven will join with delight.

OUR WORDS

How sober should we live,
  How thoughtful here below,
And all our powers of being give
  That all our Lord may know.

No room for jest or joke,
  Nor idle, careless laugh,
While sinners by death's whirlwind stroke
  Are carried off as chaff.

But earnest, sober words,
  Seasoned with salt of grace,
Well pleasing to our risen Lord
  If spoken face to face.

Oh, let our words declare,
  That we our Savior know,
And heavenly thoughts find echo there,
  And heavenly blessings flow.

CALL FOR REAPERS

Reaper, wherefore dost thou linger,
  Harvest fields are ripe to-day,
And the Master loudly calleth;
  Hasten, reaper, while you may.

Great the work and few the workers,
  Work increases, workmen fall;
Gird thee for the day of labor,
  Haste thee at thy Master's call.

Hast thou fears of men's opinions?
  Do thy friends retard thy way?
Art thou seeking, vainly seeking,
  For thy soul some earthly stay?

Storm clouds lower yonder,
  Day declines, the end is nigh,
"Harvest past—the summer ended"
  Shall thy soul forever cry?

Ah! you answer to the summons,
  See your life's work, enter in.
Praise the Lord, no soul shall perish,
  Through thine idleness and sin.

Golden sheaves you now may garner,
  Garner safely for the skies,
And the reaper's song eternal,
  You may sing with glad surprise.

'Midst the harvest home rejoicings,
  Circled round by gathered grain,
Kindred spirits—fellow reapers,
  Swell with thee the glad refrain.

NO FACE LIKE THINE

No face like Thine, my Savior.
  Fair as the lily white,
Amid the throng that drifts along,
  Shedding a heavenly light.

CHORUS
I shall see His glorious face,
I shall see His glorious face;
And gaze upon it evermore—
My Savior's glorious face.

No face like Thine, my Savior,
  More marred than any seen,
By crown of thorn and Calvary's morn,
  The heavens and earth between.

No face like Thine, my Savior,
  Brighter than noonday sun;
For saints, 'tis light—for sinners, night.
  With work of judgment done.

No face like Thine, my Savior,
  Oh, majesty divine;
No sun, no moon, but Christ alone,
  Of heaven, the Light sublime.

THE DAY OF HIS COMING

He cometh, He cometh,
  The Judge on His throne,
With ten thousand thousands
  Redeemed for His own.

The dead are arising
  From graves opened wide,
No time for excuses,
  No coverts to hide.

The sun plunged in darkness,
  The moon dipped in blood;
All nations are wailing
  At sight of their God.

'Mid hoarse muttering thunders
  And loud roaring sea
And earthquakes confounded,
  The sinner shall be.

To saints and to angels,
  His welcome is smiled,
Come, blest of my Father,
  Through blood reconciled.

EARTH'S VANITIES

I have sought pleasure, this wide world around,
Drank its cup deeply, but none have I found.
  Sweet for a moment, then bitter as gall,
  Flash like a meteor, then darkness o'er all.
Vanities all, yea, much lighter than air,
Briars for roses, for peace, heaviest care,
  Heart-sick and weary, to whom shall I go?
  Help, or I perish; Thy mercy, Lord, show.

Friendships were mine with the fairest of earth,
Heart knit to heart of true merit and worth:
  Gone, and I'm left with the perishing clod,
  Chords snapped asunder—"Pass under the rod."
Low 'mid the ashes of sorrow I lie,
Covered with sackcloth and wishing to die.
  End of perfection, to whom shall I flee?
  Savior, have mercy; I would come to Thee.

Treadmills of duty that never are done,
Conflicts and battles, but victories none;
  Troubles like billows roll over my head,
  Fearing, yet wishing, to lie with the dead,
Wishing 'twere morning, as fast speeds the night,
Wishing 'twere evening, when breaks morning light,
  Restless and wretched, oh, must I thus roam?
  No peace, no Jesus, no hope, and no home.

My heart is weary of din and of strife,
Weary of living this unmeaning life,
  Satisfied never, no peace and no rest,
  Warring waves ever beat fierce on my breast.
Discord, confusion, wherever I go,
Life is so empty, a vanity show.
  Oh, must I ever in wretchedness sigh?
  Help me, my Savior; I perish, I die.

Hark! 'tis a voice like the waves of the sea
Breaks on my soul, with glad tidings for me,—
  "Come unto me, all ye weary and worn,
  Heavily laden, your burden I've borne.
Cast it all down at the foot of the cross,
Joy for your sorrow, and gain for your loss,
  Plenty for poverty, gladness divine."
  Lord, I am coming; oh, may I be Thine?

Gladly I yield to the mandate above,
Cast down my burden of sin for His love,
  Take up my cross, and its weight I adore
  For His dear sake, who for me the load bore.
Dead to the world, and the world unto me,
From all its follies forever set free,
  Quick as a flash comes the light all divine—
  Jesus, my Savior, I am Thine, I am Thine!

Now I have found what my soul long has craved,
Glory to Jesus, I am saved, I am saved!
  Saved from my sorrow and strivings and sin,
  Saved from my foes from without and within.
Heaven has come with its sweetness and rest,
Satisfied ever, continually blest,
  Well-springs of joy, floods of glory divine,
  Shout the glad news; Lord, eternally Thine!

THE OLD SONG EVER NEW

I have a song my heart would sing,
'Tis not of noble, lord or king,
'Tis not of beauty, gold or power,
Or fleeting joys of earthly hour,
Nor yet of self or dearest friend,
For earth's perfection hath an end.

My song is new, and yet e'er old,
On Judah's plain, by angels told
The first, and down the ages grand
It floods with glory every land.
To God be glory, praise and worth,
Good-will and peace to men on earth.

The Psalmist from the depths did cry,
"Oh, help me, Savior, or I die."
The Lord inclined His ear and heard,
And soothed his fear with gracious word;
Upon the rock made sure his feet
And in his mouth a new song sweet.

In Chaldee's land the Jews did sit
Hard by the weeping willow's feet;
Their harps upon the branches hung,
Nor praise was offered, song was sung;
By sighing winds the chords were moved,
No heart made glad, no spirit soothed.

When asked for music from their hand,
"We can not sing in this strange land;
Our heart, 'Jerusalem!' doth cry;
'For thee we pine, for thee we sigh.' "
Unless the heart be fired with song,
In vain the numbers roll along.

My heart was sad, no song for me
Did rise and fall with accents free;
My sins like mountains round me closed
And all my heavenward flight opposed;
A voice I heard, "Yea, all is done,
Ye weary, heavy-laden, come."

I listened to the timely word
And cast my burden on the Lord,
And sprang up in an endless strain,
Like ever-falling, pattering rain;
And wondered as I heard again,
"On earth good-will and peace to men."

And now joy ripples through my soul,
Then streams, then pours, till over-full;

I press, I shake, it overflows,
And to a saddened world it goes.
I'll sing my song till life shall cease,
"Good-will on earth to men, and peace."

VALIANT HEARTED SOLDIERS

O valiant hearted soldiers, of all our faithful bands,
God calls to greater labors, alike on sea and land.
In vain He shall not summon, ready to die or live;
"Send me," we answer gladly; "our all we freely give."

CHORUS
Then out, away, and onward,
To darkest heathen lands,
To take this world for Jesus;
Press on, ye valiant bands.

God-called and spirit-burdened, for service ev'rywhere,
In dark and distant countries, in line for service there.
E'en life most freely given, to rescue men from death;
And crying, "Jesus only," till life's supremest breath.

No time for lamentation, nor for the fun'ral tread;
Let those who dwell in darkness, dead souls, watch o'er their
dead.
The Master calls thee, hasten whene'er you hear His voice;
Oh, let not self or Satan, but Jesus, guide your choice.

Ten thousand sit in darkness, ten thousand stretch their
hands,
Ten thousand cry in anguish, "Oh, come and save our lands!"
Hasten, ye soldiers, blood-washed, and called of God to go,
Hasten on wings of morning, that all your Lord may know.

This, this your mission, workers, to ev'ry land and tongue:
Go, go proclaim the story, e'en as your Lord has done!
Farewell, cry as you hasten, to home, and ease, and friends:
Then forward, outward ever, till life and toil shall end.

THOUSANDS FOR JESUS

There are thousands who wander in darkness
On the perilous mountains of sin,
We will seek them with cries and entreaties,
Though our eyes may with weeping be dim.

CHORUS
We are after our thousands for Jesus,
  Our glorious, all-conquering King,
We will snatch them as brands from the burning,
  Then thousands shall victory sing.

There are thousands now dwelling sad-hearted
  In the valleys and shadows of death.
"No one cares for my soul," they are crying,
  And they sigh with their fast-hastening breath.

In the byways of ruin they wander,
  They tread on the brink of despair;
They sit with the scorners, ne'er dreaming
  That danger and death lurketh there.

The lowest and vilest downtrodden,
  In the murkiest midnight of sin,
Shall see the glad light of the Gospel,
  And with us and our King enter in.

To the cross of the uplifted Savior
  Our thousands are coming with haste,
From the mountain, the woodland, the prairie,
  The city and desolate waste.

Yes, thousands are coming; salvation
  Shall sweep like the waves of the sea;
And the songs and the shouts of rejoicing
  Shall foretell of the glad jubilee.

ONLY FOR SOULS

Only for souls, our life-work shall be;
Only for souls, till death shall set free;
We'll strive as those running after earth's goals,
Only for souls, only for souls.

CHORUS
Souls all exposed to sin's dark blight,
Souls all exposed to eternal night;
Oh, haste to the rescue, for time swiftly rolls!
Only for souls, only for souls.

Only for souls, while the tear-drops start,
Only for souls, though with aching heart;
Go, friendships and pleasures,—your death-knell tolls;
Only for souls, only for souls.

Only for souls, with zeal eaten up,
Only for souls, Gethsemane's cup,
My heart, thou the altar where burneth live coals;
Only for souls, only for souls.

Only for souls, be it far or near,
Only for souls, the summons we'll hear,
From the heat of the tropic to earth's steady poles;
Only for souls, only for souls.

Only for souls, tho' the conflict be long,
Only for souls, 'gainst an enemy strong,
Victorious the issue,—God all controls;
Only for souls, only for souls.

—Written in 1885.

THE WONDROUS CHANGE

My past of life,
How sad to me the memory!
The heartaches and the sighs,
The longing want for something always wanting;
For joy e'er seeking, yet joy fore'er pursuing,
The phantom in my grasp I sometimes seemed to have;
It vanished like the will o'wisp,
And left me gazing mournfully on gilded bubbles,
Where I'd thought was real good.
I came and went, and came again,
In empty sound of meaningless pursuit;
In search of something new to ease my aching heart.
I wandered o'er my circling course
In path so often trod,
Like beaten path of treadmill.
Recognized at last, I cried,
"My wasted days!" Life is but vanity.
No rest I found, no peace, no ease of conscience.
For like the troubled sea which can not rest,
But casteth up continually mire and dirt,
So is the wicked.

While I wondered thus like shipwrecked mariner,
Who, without compass, chart, logbook, helm, or masts,
Drifts through the pathless darkness of the deep,
A ray of light divine beamed on my darkness.
It consolation brought in words sweeter than music,
"Come unto me all ye who weary are and laden heavy,
And I will give you rest."
"Come now and let us reason, saith the Lord,
And though your sins as scarlet be, or crimson,
They shall be as white as snow."
I saw my wrong. A life of self I'd lived.
But now with all my heart I turn to Him,
Who died and rose again.
Oh! I remember well when I surrendered
All my life to God.
The peace that passeth all human understanding
Filled my soul.
I turned my vision heavenward,
And the gates of glory lifted up their heads
To let the conquerors in,
Heaven smiled, angels rejoiced,
And to its far, remotest bounds
Hell groaned Disappointment at my gain.
And now I live and yet not I,
For Christ my Savior liveth in me.
To do His will is more than meat or drink,
And morning, noon and night the dews of heaven,
Like showers of rain upon new-mown hay,
Refreshingly perfume my soul.
Oh, joy supernal! bliss unspeakable!
God is my Father, I His child,
Redeemed from death and hell;
And with my heart made pure
And garments white in His own blood
I upward press my way to gates of pearl,
And gold-paved streets;
And all the eternities of bliss
In Christ and Heaven,—
     All mine.

"The land of the living," where men breathe to sigh?
"The land of the living," where men live to die?
Where sorrow, temptation, woe, carnage and strife
Embitter and harrow our time-given life?

"A land of the living? Oh yes, that's above,
In the summertide bloom of the land of pure love;
In the land of the dying, we plow and we sow,
To the land of the living for harvest we go.

BENEDICTION

Grace and mercy. peace and love,
From the triune God above,
Be upon us while we part,
Join us each to each in heart:
Save the wandering and the lost,
Ere they pay the fearful cost,
Shed upon us each this hour,
Saving, cleansing, keeping power.

We'll Girdle the Globe With Salvation.

V. A. DAKE.   IDA M. DAKE.

1. Behold the hands......... stretched out for aid,....... Darkened by
2. In heathen lands..... ......they watch and wait, ... And sigh for
3. O flash the tid - - ings! shout the sound,......... In dark-est
4. The watchfires kin - - dle far and near,......... In ev-'ry

1. Behold the hands   stretched out for aid,
2. In heathen lands   they watch and wait,
3. O flash the tidings -   -   shout the sound,
4. The watchfires kindle   -   far and near,

sin,............. and sore dis-mayed,............ O will you
help............. which comes so late,............. And grope in
lands .... the world a-round,............. Till all the
land.............. let them ap-pear,............. Till burn-ing

Darkened by sin   and sore dismayed,
And sigh for help   which comes so late;
In dark-est lands   the world a-round,
In ev-'ry land   let them ap-pear,

to......... their rescue go, ... Lost wand'rers down to endless woe?
sin........ and nature's night,....... For-ev-er vain-ly seeking light.
earth,..... from pole to pole,........ Shall full Salvation echoes roll.
lines..... of gos-pel fire, Shall gird the world and mount up higher.

rit.

O will you to   their rescue go, Lost wand'rers down to endless woe?
And grope in sin   and nature's night, Forever vainly seeking light.
Till all the earth,   from pole to pole, Shall hear salvation's echoes roll.
Till burning lines of gospel fire, Shall gird the world and mount up higher.

CHORUS.

We'll girdle the globe with sal-va-tion, With ho-li-ness un-to the Lord:

And light shall il-lu-mine each nation, The light from the lamp of his word.

At the close of a misionary class meeting at the Seminary at North Chili, New York, February 21, 1892, where much of the Spirit's presence was manifested, while singing "We'll Girdle the Globe with Salvation," Superintendent B. T. Roberts remarked to his wife and others: "If Adelbert Dake had done nothing but write that piece, his life work would have been a success."

The numbers attached to the songs in this book refer to the numbers as they appear in the Metrical Tune Book.

310 No. 21 Let Me go to the Vineyard of God.

V. A. Dake.

Ida M. Dake.

1. Let me go, let me go to the vine-yard of God Let me
2. Let me go, let me go to the low-est of earth. Sink-ing
3. Let me go, let me go, till the sheaves are all bound, And are

go and for-ev-er a-bide; Ev-er val-iant and strong in the
down in their filth and their sin; For my Saviour has shown me their
meet for the gar-ner on high; Till the Lord of the har-vest shall

work of the Lord, Working close by the cru ci-fied side. Let me
in-fi-nite worth, And I has-ten my work to be-gin. What tho'
say, "I have found all my sheaves for the sweet by and by." Let me

go, tell the world I am dead to its charms, For my friends ring a
death I see oft! What tho' per-ils are mine! I am strong in the
go, let me go, Till I've crossed the cold stream, And have joined the re-

fi-nal death knell; From the vine-yard of God I have
might of the Lord; And I has-ten to join in the
deemed on the shore; Till I've swept thro' the gate like the

heard the a-larm, Work to do, dear-est i-dols, fare-well.
work so di-vine, And I con-quer by his might-y word.
lightning's bright gleam, And I gaze on my Christ ev-er-more.

DIP YOUR FOOT IN OIL

Deuteronomy 33:24

If your path in life is weary,
  Dip your foot in oil.
If your days are dark and dreary,
  Dip your foot in oil.
'Twill make your pathway lighten,
'Twill make your dark days brighten,
'Twill from you sad cares frighten—
  Then dip your foot in oil.

CHORUS
Then dip your foot in oil,
'Twill lighten all your toil,
  'Twill smooth rough ways,
  Brighten dark days—
Then dip your foot in oil.

If to peace you are a stranger,
  Dip your foot in oil.
If your end seems full of danger,
  Dip your foot in oil.
Peace like a mighty river
Shall fill your soul forever,
And death shall bring no quiver—
  Then dip your foot in oil.

If you wish a joy undying,
  Dip your foot in oil.
And a lifetime free from sighing,
  Dip your foot in oil.
Your heart to pour forth singing,
Your notes of victory ringing,
Your feet toward heaven springing—
  Then dip your foot in oil.

No. 36 # I Will Rejoice.

V. A. DAKE.

IDA M. DAKE.

1. Tho' flocks and herds may per-ish, And fields may yield no store;
2. Tho' per - se - cu - tion com - eth, A fierce and venge-ful roar,
3. Tho' fee - ble, faint and suf-f'ring, With bur - dens la - den sore,
4. For God him-self commandeth, I wait to hear no more,
5. Then on thro' ev - 'ry con - flict, Till gleams the heav'n-ly shore.

Tho' friends should all for-sake me,
Of hate, re-proach and scorning,
I'll shout till breaks the dawning,
But run to do his bid-ding,
And an - gels join the cho - rus.
} I will rejoice ev - er-more.

CHORUS.

I will re - joice, I will re - joice, Tho'
I will rejoice, I will rejoice,

men and dev - ils roar, I will re - joice, I will re -
I will rejoice,

joice, I will re-joice ev - er - more.
I will rejoice,

VIVIAN A. DAKE.   FLORA BIRDSALL NELSON.

1. There's a world ev-er-last-ing, Of jas-per and pearl;
2. There's a house ev-er-last-ing, Not build-ed with hands,
3. There's a crown ev-er-last-ing, A crown of pure gold,

And o-nyx and ber-yl, And dia-mond and gold; And
Nor found-ed on sand, But built on the rock, Where
And stars, I am told, If lost ones I bring, To the

glo-ry un-told, And there I shall dwell, ev - er dwell.
com-eth no shock, And there is my home, ne'er to roam.
feet of my King, That crown I shall wear, ev - er wear.

Ev- er dwell,   ev- er dwell,   And there I shall dwell, ever dwell.
Ne'er to roam,   ne'er to roam,   And there is my home, ne'er to roam.
Ev- er wear,   ev- er wear,   That crown I shall wear, ever wear.

Ev- er dwell,   ev- er dwell,
Ne'er to roam,   ne'er to roam,
Ev- er wear,   ev- er wear,

4 There's a hymn everlasting,
The Lamb is the theme,
So strong to redeem,
A hymn never old,
And yet ever told,
That hymn I shall sing, for my King.
REF.—For my King, etc.

5 There's a King everlasting,
He comes on his throne,
His children to own,
They waited full long,
With prayer and with song,
And now he has come, welcome home.
REF.—Welcome home, etc.

Lost in sight of Home.

V. A. D.   V. A. DAKE.

1. Long in far off coun-tries Has the good ship been; Man-y storm-waves
2. Fiercely roars the tem-pest, Round a help-less bark, Struggling with the
3. Souls of men, who tri-fle With e-ter-nal things, Thinking not of
4. Seen are heav-en's coast-lines, But the fur-ious gale Beats in all its

breast-ed, Man-y dan-gers seen; Now all hearts are hope-ful,
break-ers, And the storm-clouds dark; Hope, from ev-'ry bos-om
dan-ger, Till it lurk-ing springs, See your doom fore-shad-owed;
mad-ness, Rend-ing ev-'ry sail; Bursts of end-less sor-row

Dis-tant shore-lines loom. And all tongues are singing, "Home, in sight of home."
Ev-er-more is gone; Loud the breakers thunder, "Lost in sight of home."
Unwarn'd shall it come, And the mournful ending, "Lost in sight of home?"
From the lost ones come; Mutt'ring thunders ech-o, "Lost in sight of home."

CHORUS.

Sad, in-deed to per-ish, While we dis-tant roam,

Sad-der for the wan-d'rer, lost in sight of home.

Eternity's Beggar.

Vivian A. Dake.
Fannie Birdsall

1. A rich man was he, and his acres were broad, And his barns he tore
2. He looked all a-ghast at the sound of that voice, And gazed on his
3. Out, out from his man sion he wandered a - way, To the depths of e

down to build more; "But thy soul is required, thou fool," said his God,
rich, earthly store; But it melt - ed a-way; he had made a sad choice,
ter - ni - ty's night, To beg for re - lief, and to long for the day,

Then to whom shall thy goods be re-stored? }
He was pov - er - ty's slave ev - er more. } E - ter - ni - ty's beg-gar!
Which shall gladden, no never, his sight. }

CHORUS.

the call he had heard, But the warning, he turned it away. O sinner!

then list to the voice of thy God, And turn to the Lord while you may.

He is Coming.

V. A. D.   V. A. DAKE.

1. He is com-ing, he   is com-ing, Can you read   the signs a - far?
2. He is com-ing, he   is com-ing, All his foes   to o - ver-throw;
3. He is com-ing, he   is com-ing, Oh! the awe - in-spir-ing sight,
4. He is com-ing, he   is com-ing, For the sigh - ing and oppressed,
5. He is com-ing, he   is com-ing, And our eyes   our King shall see;

Do you   hear the tread of na-tions, As they march to join in war?
And the hid - den plots of dark-ness, All the   u - ni-verse shall know;
With the blasts of judgment trumpets, He is   com - ing in his might.
And the long - ing eyes shall see him, And the wea - ry ones shall rest.
Long has been the time of watching, But he's com - ing aft - er me.

Do you   hear the gos- pel her - ald, Call-ing loud   in ev - 'ry land?
O'er his en - e-mies tri - um-phant, He shall reign up-on his throne;
He   is com - ing on the lightning, With his bright an-gel - ic cloud;
Hear the fall - ing of the fet- ters, And tbe crash of op'ning graves;
Floods of joy with-in are bursting, As I   catch his glorious smile;

O, ye   na-tions, turn, re-pent ye, For his   coming   is   at hand.
Ev -'ry knee be - fore him bending, Him, the mighty God shall own.
Mid the roar of might-y earthquakes, And ten thousand thunders loud.
O-ver-thrown is death's dominions, Shout! ye saints, no lon - ger slaves.
He is   com-ing, quick - ly com-ing, He is coming   for his child.

CHORUS.

Watch for his com-ing, watch for his com-ing,

Watch for the hour draweth near; Soon thro' the dawning, will

burst e-ter-nal morning, And the Lord to greet his faithful will ap-pear.

AT EASE IN ZION

At ease in Zion! wo to those
Who in their sins idly repose,
And sing the songs of worldly mirth,
Forgetful of their Savior's worth.

At ease in Zion! wo to thee,
The trumphet sounds! Awake and flee,
Nor rest in such a dangerous state,
Lest thou should'st wake at last—too late.

At ease in Zion, while the lost
Upon the waves of strife are tossed,
And loud they call, "Ho, brother, save!
Oh, snatch us from the yawning grave."

At ease in Zion, wo at last,
The harvest o'er, the summer past;
With fires devouring you must dwell,
'Mid everlasting flames in hell.

VIVIAN A. DAKE.   IDA M. DAKE.

1. "I've miss'd it at last," he re-peat-ed,   While the shades of de

2. "The thief on the cross I re-mem-ber,   Ne'er re-fused till the

3. "I've sold out my soul for a feath-er,   No hope in the

4. "The spir-it in-sult-ed, re-sist-ed,   Still plead till the

5. He bur-ied his face in the pil-low,   With hor-ror his

spair gathered fast; "My hopes are for-ev-er de-feat-ed, I have missed,

sum-mer was past, And now in death's chilling December, I have missed,

whirlwind's fierce blast, I'm undone for-ev-er and ev-er, I have missed,

die I had cast, I said 'Go thy way,' I in-sist-ed; He went,

soul all a-ghast, And back from e-ter-ni-ty's bil-low, He shriek'd

CHORUS.

I have missed it at last!" "I've missed it at last, missed salva-tion,

From the pure and the ho-ly out-cast; Nev-er-more peace—to

ad lib.

feel dire dam-na-tion—I've missed, I have missed it at last."

Mighty Trump.

Arr. by VIVIAN A. DAKE.   Arr. by FANNIE BIRDSALL.

1. He com-eth! he com-eth! The Judge on his throne,
2. The dead are all ris-ing, From graves o-pened wide;
3. The sun plunged in dark-ness; The moon dipped in blood;
4. 'Mid hoarse, mut-t'ring thun-der, And loud roar-ing seas,

With ten thou-sand thou-sand Re-deemed for His own.
No time for ex-cus-es, No cov-erts to hide.
All na-tions are wail-ing At sight of their God.
With earth-quakes, con-found-ed, The sin-ner will be.

CHORUS.

When the might-y, might-y, might-y trump Sounds "Come, come a-

way," Oh, may we be read-y To hail that glad day.

5 To saints and to angels
   His welcome is smiled,
"Come, blessed of my Father,
   Thro' blood reconciled."

6 When soundeth the trumpet,
   And breaks judgment light,
Oh, I shall be ready,
   With garments washed white.

352 No. 62 **Thousands for Jesus.**

Vivian A. Dake. Fannie Birdsall.

1. There are thou-sands who wander in dark - ness, On the per - il - ous
2. There are thou-sands now dwelling sad-hearted, In the val - leys and
3. In the by - ways of ru - in they wan - der, They tread on the
4. The low - est and vil - est down trodden, In the murk - i - est

moun-tains of sin, We will seek them with cries and en-treat - ies,
shad - ows of death, "No one cares for my soul," they are cry - ing,
brink of de-spair, They sit with the scorners, ne'er dreaming,
mid-night of sin, Shall see the glad light of the Gos - pel,

CHORUS.

Tho' our eyes may with weep-ing be dim.
And they sigh with their fast hast'ning breath.
That dan - ger and death lurk-eth there.
And with us and our King en - ter in.
We are af - ter our

thousands for Je - sus, Our glo-rious, all - con-quer-ing King, We will

snatch them as brands from the burning, Then thousands shall victory sing

Copyright, 1891, by V. A. Dake.

222

5 To the cross of the uplifted Saviour,
Our thousands are coming with haste,
From the mountain, the woodland, the prairie,
The city and desolate waste.

6 Yes, thousands are coming; salvation
Shall sweep like the waves of the sea;
And the songs and the shouts of rejoicing,
Shall foretell of the glad jubilee.

63 Confess Your Sins.

V. A. DAKE.　　　　　　　　　　FANNIE BIRDSALL.

1. Would you know the Spirit's pow'r? Would you feel it ev-'ry hour?
2. Would you know your sins forgiv'n? Would you have each i-dol riv'n?
3. Would you o-ver-come each day? Shout the vic-t'ry on your way?
4. Would you work till lat-est breath? Sing tri-umph-ant o-ver death?

Would you have a heart made white? One that Je-sus says is right?
Would you ease your bur-dened soul? From your day the darkness roll?
In each tri-al bright-er shine? Nev-er mur-mur or re-pine?
Meet thy God with rec-ord clear? Then par-take of end-less cheer?

CHORUS.

Con-fess your sins to Je-sus, Make right your ev'ry
Con-fess your sins to Je-sus, Make right your

wrong; Dig deep and strike the fountain, Which turns thy sighs to song.
ev-'ry wrong;

Copyright, 1891, by V. A. Dake.

223